# RISE & SHINE

# OAT Prep
# Grade 8 Reading Comprehension

by Jonathan D. Kantrowitz

Edited by Patricia F. Braccio and Sarah M.W. Espano

Item Code RAS 2065 • Copyright © 2009 Queue, Inc.

All rights reserved. No part of the material protected by this copyright may be reproduced or utilized in any form or by any means, electronic or mechanical, including photocopying, recording, or by any information storage and retrieval system. Printed in the United States of America.

Queue, Inc. • 80 Hathaway Drive, Stratford, CT 06615
(800) 232-2224 • Fax: (800) 775-2729 • www.qworkbooks.com

# Table of Contents

**To the Students** .................................................. v
from "Trifles" *by Susan Glaspell* ........................... 1
"Future Scientist" ...................................................... 7
Preserving the Present: Time Capsules .............. 11
Chile: The Long Road of Change ........................ 17
Jumbo ........................................................................ 23
from *Tarzan of the Apes* ...................................... 27
　*by Edgar Rice Burroughs*
Seat Belts .................................................................. 31
from *The Call of the Wild* ..................................... 35
　*by Jack London*
Communication ....................................................... 39
Ralph Nader ............................................................. 43
from *Tarzan of the Apes—Part II* ....................... 47
　*by Edgar Rice Burroughs*
Kristine Lilly ............................................................ 51
Sengbe Pieh (Cinque)—Capture, Revolt, and
　Recapture ............................................................. 53
The Complicated Life of a
　Patuxent Whooper Egg ..................................... 57
from *A Fancy of Hers* ............................................ 61
　*by Horatio Alger*
from *A Fancy of Hers—Part II* .............................. 65
　*by Horatio Alger*
from *Peter Pan by J.M. Barrie* ............................. 69
from "Negro Schoolmaster in the New South" .. 73
　*by W.E.B. DuBois*
Soy Protein .............................................................. 75
The Captive *by John R. Musick* ........................... 79
Harry and His Dog .................................................. 83
　*by Mary Russell Mitford*
from *The Golden Touch* ........................................ 87
　*by Nathaniel Hawthorne*
from *The Velveteen Rabbit* ................................... 91
　*by Margery Williams Bianco*
Cesar Chavez .......................................................... 95
Earth's Water ........................................................... 99
Traveling Abroad .................................................. 103
Censorship in Music ............................................. 107
from *The Financier* ............................................... 113
　*by Theodore Dreiser*
Poison Ivy and Its Cousins .................................. 125
James P. Beckwourth, Black
　Mountain Man ................................................... 129
African Americans in Combat ............................. 133
from *The Red-Headed League* ........................... 135
　*by Arthur Conan Doyle*

The Quest for Happiness ..................................... 139
　FROM "DELICATESSEN"
　　*by Joyce Kilmer*
　"YOUNG LOCHINVAR"
　　*by Sir Walter Scott*
"Get Up and Bar the Door" ................................. 145
"The Men that Don't Fit In" ................................. 149
　*by Robert W. Service*
"Harriet Beecher Stowe" ..................................... 153
　*by Paul Laurence Dunbar*
Excerpted from "The Pied Piper of Hamelin,
　A Child's Story" ................................................ 157
　*by Robert Browning*
from "Hiawatha's Childhood" .............................. 161
　*by Henry Wadsworth Longfellow*
from "The Rime of the Ancient Mariner" .......... 167
　*by Samuel Taylor Coleridge*
"Two Moods from the Hill" ................................. 173
　*by Ernest Benshimol*
"The Planting of the Apple Tree" ....................... 177
　*by William Cullen Bryant*
American Indian Settlement in Ohio ................. 181
European Settlements in Ohio .......................... 185
Climate and Weather ........................................... 189
The Western Reserve and the
　Cuyahoga Valley ............................................... 193
Ohio Wars ............................................................... 197
Ohio State Symbols ............................................. 203
Migration to Ohio, 1785–1850 ........................... 207
Canal and Railroad ............................................... 211
Ohio Women .......................................................... 215
Earthquakes and Seismic Risk in Ohio ............ 221
John Parker of Ripley, Ohio ................................ 227
Immigration and Ethnic Heritage in Ohio ........ 231
Muskellunge Fishing in Ohio .............................. 237
Agriculture in Ohio ................................................ 243
Temperance and Prohibition in Ohio ................ 247
Improving Lake Erie ............................................. 251
Entertainment and Leisure Activities ................ 255
Women's Rights in Ohio ...................................... 259
Sports in Ohio ........................................................ 263
Running Buffalo Clover ........................................ 269
From Bicycles to Airplanes ................................. 273
Alphonso and William Howard Taft .................. 277
Lake Erie Water Snake ........................................ 283
The Ohio Memory Online Scrapbook ............... 287
Teays River ............................................................ 293

# To the Students

### Tips for Answering Multiple-Choice Questions

Multiple-choice questions each have a **stem**, which is a question or incomplete sentence, followed by four answer choices. You should select only one answer choice. The following are some tips to help you correctly answer multiple-choice questions on the Ohio Grade 8 Reading Achievement Test:

- Read each selection carefully.
- Read each question and think about how best to answer. You may look back to the reading selection as often as necessary.
- Answer all questions on your answer sheet. Do not mark any answers to questions in your test booklet.
- For each question, choose the best answer, and completely fill in the circle in the space provided on your answer sheet.
- If you do not know the answer to a question, skip it and go on. You may return to it later if you have time.
- If you finish the section of the test that you are working on early, you may review your answers in that section only. Don't go on to the next section of the test.

### Tips for Answering Short-Answer and Extended-Response Questions

Remember to:

- Read the question carefully. Be sure you understand it before you begin writing.
- Be sure your answer has a main idea. This should be in your introduction.
- Support your main idea with details, explanations, and examples.
- State your ideas in a clear sequence.
- Include an opening and a closing.
- Use a variety of words and vary your sentence structure.
- Check your spelling, capitalization, and punctuation.
- Write neatly.

# from "TRIFLES"
## by Susan Glaspell

1 *This play involves a murder mystery. Who killed Mr. Wright? In this excerpt from the play, two men are in the Wright home, investigating the crime. The men's wives have accompanied them. As the men search for hard evidence, the women consider the subtle elements of the case and the relationship between Mr. and Mrs. Wright.*

2 **MRS. PETERS.** (*Glancing around.*) Seems funny to think of a bird here. But she must have had one, or why should she have a cage? I wonder what happened to it.

3 **MRS. HALE.** I s'pose maybe the cat got it.

4 **MRS. PETERS.** No, she didn't have a cat. She's got that feeling some people have about cats—being afraid of them. My cat got in her room, and she was real upset and asked me to take it out.

5 **MRS. HALE.** My sister Bessie was like that. Queer, ain't it?

6 **MRS. PETERS.** (*Examining the cage.*) Why, look at this door. It's broke. One hinge is pulled apart.

7 **MRS. HALE.** (*Looking, too.*) Looks as if someone must have been rough with it.

8 **MRS. PETERS.** Why, yes. (*She brings the cage forward and puts it on the table.*)

9 **MRS. HALE.** I wish if they're going to find any evidence they'd be about it. I don't like this place.

10 **MRS. PETERS.** But I'm awful glad you came with me, Mrs. Hale. It would be lonesome for me sitting here alone.

11 **MRS. HALE.** It would, wouldn't it? (*Dropping her sewing.*) But I tell you what I do wish, Mrs. Peters. I wish I had come over sometimes she was here. I—(*Looking around the room.*)—wish I had.

12 **MRS. PETERS.** But of course you were awful busy, Mrs. Hale—your house and your children.

13 **MRS. HALE.** I could've come. I stayed away because it weren't cheerful—and that's why I ought to have come. I—I've never liked this place. Maybe because it's down in a hollow, and you don't see the road. I dunno what it is but it's a lonesome place and always was. I wish I had come over to see Minnie Foster[1] sometimes. I can see now—(*Shakes her head.*)

14 **MRS. PETERS.** Well, you mustn't reproach yourself, Mrs. Hale. Somehow we just don't see how it is with other folks until—something comes up.

15   **MRS. HALE.** Not having children makes less work—but it makes a quiet house, and Wright out to work all day, and no company when he did come in. Did you know John Wright, Mrs. Peters?

16   **MRS. PETERS.** Not to know him; I've seen him in town. They say he was a good man.

17   **MRS. HALE.** Yes—good; he didn't drink, and kept his word as well as most, I guess, and paid his debts. But he was a hard man, Mrs. Peters. Just to pass the time of day with him—(*Shivers.*) Like a raw wind that gets to the bone. (*Pauses, her eye falling on the cage.*) I should think she would 'a wanted a bird. But what do you suppose went with it?

18   **MRS. PETERS.** I don't know, unless it got sick and died. (*She reaches over and swings the broken door, swings it again, both women watch it.*)

19   **MRS. HALE.** You weren't raised round here, were you? (*Mrs. Peters shakes her head.*) You didn't know—her?

20   **MRS. PETERS.** Not till they brought her yesterday.

21   **MRS. HALE.** She—come to think of it, she was kind of like a bird herself—real sweet and pretty, but kind of timid and—fluttery. How—she—did—change. (*Silence; then as if struck by a happy thought and relieved to get back to everyday things.*) Tell you what, Mrs. Peters, why don't you take the quilt in with you? It might take up her mind.

22   **MRS. PETERS.** Why, I think that's a real nice idea, Mrs. Hale. There couldn't possible be any objection to it, could there? Now, just what would I take? I wonder if her patches are in here—and her things. (*They look in the sewing basket.*)

23   **MRS. HALE.** Here's some red. I expect this has got sewing things in it. (*Brings out a fancy box.*) What a pretty box. Looks like something somebody would give you. Maybe her scissors are in here. (*Opens box. Suddenly puts her hand to her nose.*) Why—(*Mrs. Peters bends nearer, then turns her face away.*) There's something wrapped up in this piece of silk.

24   **MRS. PETERS.** Why, this isn't her scissors.

25   **MRS. HALE** (*lifting the silk*). Oh, Mrs. Peters—it's—(*Mrs. Peters bends closer.*)

26   **MRS. PETERS.** It's the bird.

[1] **Minnie Foster** is Mrs. Wright's maiden name.

1. What was Mrs. Hale's main problem in the passage?

   A. She wanted to find out what happened to Mr. Wright.
   B. She was trying to figure out who killed the bird.
   C. She wished that she could do something for Mrs. Wright.
   D. She did not like being in Mrs. Wright's house.

This question asks you about the main problem in the passage. Sometimes, readers confuse supporting details with the main problem. To find the main problem, look at each answer choice and pick the problem that the character struggles with for the entire passage. The two women hardly ever mentioned what happened to Mr. Wright in the passage (answer choice A). Until the end of the passage, the women didn't even know that the bird was dead, so answer choice B is incorrect. Mrs. Hale mentioned that life must have been hard for Mrs. Wright and she wished that she could have done something for her, so answer choice C may be correct. Answer choice D suggests that Mrs. Hale's main problem was that she didn't like being in the house. Mrs. Hale did mention this feeling, but it was not her main problem. Answer choice C is correct.


2. Mrs. Hale would most likely agree with which statement about Mr. Wright?

   A. He was very dishonest.
   B. He was coldhearted to his wife.
   C. He was generous to others.
   D. He was very popular.

In the passage, Mrs. Hale tells Mrs. Peters about Mr. Wright. Think back to their conservation. Did Mrs. Hale suggest he was dishonest (answer choice A)? No, she said that he probably acted fairly and told the truth. Mrs. Hale also does not say that he was generous to other people (answer choice C) or that he was very popular (answer choice D). The best answer is answer choice B. Mr. Wright was coldhearted to his wife.

3. According to the passage, what did Mrs. Hale regret?

   A. introducing herself to Mrs. Peters
   B. joining her husband at the Wright home
   C. not visiting Mrs. Wright in the past
   D. not helping Mr. Hale with his job

   In the passage, Mrs. Hale revealed regret for the way she acted. She was not upset about having introduced herself to Mrs. Peters (answer choice A), since the two are good friends. Mrs. Hale did not mention her decision to join her husband on the case (answer choice B), and she did not show any motivation to help him with his job (answer choice D). She regretted not having visited the lonely Mrs. Wright. Answer choice C is best.

4. Which statement best describes Mrs. Hale and Mrs. Peters' view of Mrs. Wright?

   A. They are critical of Mrs. Wright's personality.
   B. They are sensitive to Mrs. Wright's situation.
   C. They feel hopeful for Mrs. Wright's future.
   D. They often competed with Mrs. Wright.

   Think back to the passage you just read. What sort of characters were Mrs. Hale and Mrs. Peters? What did they say and how did they act? They did not seem critical of Mrs. Wright (answer choice A); instead, they seemed to feel sorry for her. They were definitely sensitive to Mrs. Wright's situation (answer choice B), so this may be the correct answer. Answer choice C is not correct. They don't seem hopeful for her future. And, while they felt sorry for Mrs. Wright, they weren't in competition with her (answer choice D). Answer choice B is the best answer.

5. "Well, you mustn't **reproach** yourself, Mrs. Hale."

   What does the word **reproach** mean?

   A. help
   B. blame
   C. thank
   D. brag

   This question asks you to figure out what a word means based on how it is used in the passage. You can use other words around the vocabulary word for clues. Mrs. Peters is talking to Mrs. Hale. Answer choice A does not make sense because Mrs. Hale didn't help herself to anything. Mrs. Hale seemed to feel bad about not visiting Mrs. Wright so answer choice B looks like a good choice. You should read every answer before marking your answer sheet, however. Answer choice C is wrong because Mrs. Hale did not sound like she was speaking well of herself. Nor was Mrs. Hale bragging because she felt badly that she did not visit Mrs. Wright. Answer choice D is incorrect. Answer choice B is the best answer.

6. According to Mrs. Hale, Mrs. Wright was like a bird because she was

   A. pretty and timid
   B. an excellent singer
   C. proud of her appearance
   D. trapped in a small room

   According to Mrs. Hale, Mrs. Wright was similar to a bird. This question asks you why Mrs. Hale made this unusual comparison. There was no mention of singing (answer choice B) in the passage excerpt, so this probably isn't the correct answer. Answer choice C does not seem to have anything to do with the passage. Mrs. Wright did seem trapped in a small room (answer choice D) like a bird in a cage, but Mrs. Hale did not make that connection. She thought that Mrs. Wright was like a bird because she was pretty, but often scared (answer choice A).

7. What did Mrs. Hale and Mrs. Peters find in the sewing basket?

   A. scissors
   B. an unfinished quilt
   C. a bird
   D. a cage

This question asks about a detail in the passage. Think back to the end of the passage. When the women opened the sewing basket, what did they find? They looked in the basket to find a pair of scissors (answer choice A), but they didn't actually locate one. The quilt that Mrs. Wright was making (answer choice B) was not in the basket. The empty bird cage (answer choice D) was hanging on the wall; it was not in the basket either. The best answer is answer choice C; there was a bird in the basket.

# "FUTURE SCIENTIST"

My shelves are covered with beakers and slides,
My desk with a scientific text
On Newton's laws of gravity,
Which I can't wait to study next.

My locker at school is filled to the brim
With ideas for several experiments
And my book is wrapped in a cover I made
From the periodic table of elements.

You see, I fell for science at a very young age
When I planted flowers outside my window
Where, with plenty of sun and a sprinkle of rain,
They sprouted and continued to grow.

It was amazing to me that life could spring
From a dirt-filled terracotta pot
And from that point on my science book became
The only book I never forgot.

I read about seeds and leaves and cells
And roots and pollination
And how plants keep cool by releasing water
Through a process called transpiration.

When I finished with plants, I turned the page
And read about the sun, moon, and stars
And it wasn't long before my telescope
Was aimed toward the planet Mars.

After the solar system I studied the Earth
From the air to the land to the seas
And learned about rocks and how mountains form
And why the polar ice caps might unfreeze.

I discovered that plates within Earth's crust
Slide along, get stuck, and then break
And cause the ground to tremble and roll
And create a giant earthquake.

The next unit I studied was all about genes,
And not the kind that you wear,
But rather the ones that determine the look
Of your nose and your eyes and your hair.

I learned about the musculoskeletal system,
The bones that help us stand up straight
And the muscles that offer the strength that we need
To run, jump, swim, and ambulate.

Blood, I read, is pumped by the heart
Into vessels called arteries
And reaches tissues and organs
Through the walls of capillaries.

Curie, Einstein, Watson, Crick,[1]
And other scientific giants
Are not only the heroes that I adore,
But the developers of modern science.

Their discoveries have kept me reading
Through my science book
And have made me pause a time or two
To have a second look.

Because of them I'll keep on reading
So my love for this subject endures
And maybe one day I'll be a scientist, too,
And find new species, planets, or cures.

[1] Marie **Curie**—made advances in radiation; Albert **Einstein**—discovered the theory of relativity; James **Watson** and Francis **Crick**—figured out the structure of DNA

1. What does the narrator use to cover his science book?

   A. diagrams of the planets
   B. pages from other books
   C. pictures of his scientific heroes
   D. the periodic table of elements

   This question asks you to recall a detail from the poem. Think back to where the narrator talks about the cover he made for his science book. What made this cover special? While he did study planets, the cover was not a diagram of them (answer choice A). There is no mention of other books that he might have used (answer choice B). The narrator does talk about scientific heroes, but he doesn't talk about having pictures of them (answer choice C). However, he does say that he used a periodic table to make a book cover (answer choice D).

2. Which word best describes the narrator of this poem?

   A. careless
   B. intrigued
   C. ambitious
   D. upset

   Think about the narrator of the poem. Whether or not you have realized it, by reading his words you've learned a lot about what kind of a person he is. Does he seem careless (answer choice A)? Not really; he seems to put a lot of care into what he is doing. Is he intrigued (answer choice B)? He is. Is he ambitious (answer choice C)? He might be, but answer choice B is a better answer. He is not upset about science (answer choice D), but he's definitely excited and intrigued by it. Answer choice B is correct.

3. "And the muscles that offer the strength that we need / To run, jump, swim, and **ambulate**."

   What does the word **ambulate** mean?

   A. walk
   B. drink
   C. pass
   D. read

   This question asks you to use the context of a line from the poem to determine the meaning of an unknown word. Read the line carefully. Think about the words that come before the unknown word. What do these words have in common? They are all action words that deal with the ways in which people move. They do not talk about drinking (answer choice B), and in this line nothing is being passed (answer choice C). Although the narrator does a lot of reading (answer choice D) this line deals more with muscles and movement. The best answer is answer choice A. The word meanings match well: run, jump, swim, and *walk*.

4. Why does the narrator of the poem begin studying science?

   A. He watches plants grow in pots of dirt.
   B. He reads a book about Albert Einstein.
   C. He is fascinated by the solar system.
   D. He learns a lot about science in school.

   The narrator talks about many of his scientific studies in the poem. However, a single one started his passion for science. Think about the event that made him become interested in science. There is no mention of a book about Einstein (answer choice B), and the narrator's fascination with the solar system (answer choice C) did not begin until after he had started studying science. The narrator does study science in school (answer choice D), but he says that he actually started "at a very young age" when he watched plants grow. Answer choice A is correct.

5. Describe how the narrator's interest in science begins and develops as he learns more. Use information from the poem to support your answer.

This question asks about the causes and effects of the narrator's passion for science. To answer this question, you'll need to write one or more paragraphs. You can look back to the poem to find all the information you need to write your answer. Think about what first causes the narrator's interest, and then trace his development as he learns about new topics. Finally, tell what he hopes to accomplish with all of his learning.

*One possible answer:*

*In the poem, the narrator first becomes involved with science when he plants some flowers in pots of dirt. As he watches them grow, he becomes fascinated by plants and begins to read about them in his science book.*

*After that, he moves on to another chapter, this one about the solar system. Then, he reads about the features of the Earth, and finally about the human body. After all of his study, he has found heroes in scientists like Curie and Einstein and he, too, wants to become a scientist.*

# PRESERVING THE PRESENT: TIME CAPSULES

1   PEOPLE OF THE PRESENT know about past cultures from discoveries of documents and artifacts that have been either accidentally or intentionally preserved. Archaeologists[1] and anthropologists[2] have dedicated countless hours to unearthing and restoring these artifacts in order to piece together the history of humankind. Consider how much easier this job would be today if past peoples had had the foresight to create time capsules to aid our understanding of their cultures.

2   A time capsule is a container that holds documents and objects that represent a culture at a certain point in time. Time capsules are designed to enable future generations to view the preserved artifacts and documents to help them understand the cultural elements of past societies.

3   The first large-scale time capsule was created by the Westinghouse Electric Corporation and displayed at the 1939 World's Fair in New York City, an event that allowed companies from all over the world to exhibit their newest and greatest ideas and inventions. Engineers at the corporation were challenged to create a vessel that would be able to preserve its contents for thousands of years. These engineers designed a material called Cupaloy that was as strong as steel and as resistant to corrosion as copper.

4   The 800-pound, missile-shaped vessel was then filled with a very thick glass tube containing about thirty-five objects specially chosen by a committee to represent life at that time, including a dollar bill, a baseball, a fountain pen, eyeglasses, a wrist watch, a toothbrush, a deck of cards, and a Mickey Mouse cup.

5   The committee also included a variety of seeds, fabrics, metals, and other manufactured materials that they thought might not exist in the distant future. In addition, a reel of microfilm containing text from newspapers, magazines, and books was also preserved in order to present future peoples with an ample understanding of life in the 1930s. While the project was interesting and entertaining, it also suggests that people understood how quickly the world was changing and how different things would be in the future.

6   On September 28, 1938, the capsule was lowered into an underground, glass-lined chamber in Flushing Meadows Park, located in Queens, New York. A document called the *Book of Record* was then created to allow people of the future to find and unearth the capsule 5,000 years later. It contains a detailed description of the burial site and the contents of the capsule, as well as a key to the English language in case it is no longer used in the year 6939. About 3,000 copies of the *Book of Record* were printed on special paper using ink that is designed to last throughout time. These copies were then distributed to libraries and archival collections all over the world.

7   In 1965, after recognizing the rapid development of society since the first time capsule had been buried, Westinghouse created a second time capsule to document these drastic changes. This second capsule contains items such as a credit card, a

record by the musical group the Beatles, a ballpoint pen, contact lenses, an electronic watch, an electric toothbrush, and a transistor radio, as well as newly developed medicines and scientific instruments. This second time capsule was buried beside the first. The site is marked with a concrete pillar that explains what lies beneath.

8   Since the idea first originated, many people have created their own time capsules to preserve elements of their personal lives. Today, the Internet makes it possible for people all over the world to document where their time capsules are buried so that future peoples can find them. Though no one can be sure that this method of preserving history will be effective, it will most likely enable people of the future to understand more than we are presently able to about our ancestors.

[1]**archaeologist**: scientist who studies the material remains of past human life and activities

[2]**anthropologist**: scientist who studies the origins and social elements of human cultures, past and present

1. The author most likely wrote this passage in order to
   A. convince readers to buy time capsules
   B. explain the development of the first time capsule
   C. entertain with a story about a famous time capsule
   D. inform readers about two large time capsules

This question asks you to identify the author's intended purpose. To answer this question, think about what the author is trying to communicate to the reader by writing this passage. The passage isn't persuasive (answer choice A). It does inform readers about two very large time capsules (answer choice D). It discusses more than just the first time capsule, so answer choice B is not the best answer. It is not a story meant to entertain (answer choice C). Answer choice D is the best answer.

2. "Consider how much easier this job would be today if past peoples had had the **foresight** to create time capsules to aid in our understanding of their cultures."

   What does the word **foresight** mean?

   A. learning ability
   B. deserving respect
   C. ability to think ahead
   D. making tools

   This question asks you to figure out the meaning of a word from the context of the sentence. Since the reader does not yet know what is required to make a time capsule, readers should not assume that past people lacked the ability to do so (answer choice A). There is nothing in this sentence—or in the sentences surrounding this sentence—to suggest that past peoples were not respectful, so answer choice B is not the best answer. The passage does not go into detail about the tools that were used to create the time capsule, which indicates that answer choice D is not the correct answer. The author is stating that it would have been easier for present-day people to understand more about cultures of the past if the people of those cultures had thought ahead and preserved their artifacts in time capsules. Answer choice C is the best answer.

3. The *Book of Record* was designed to

   A. help people of the future find the time capsule
   B. explain the uses of each item in the time capsule
   C. provide people with text from 1930s books and papers
   D. amuse future peoples with stories of the past

   This question asks you about a detail from the passage. The answer to this question is stated in the passage. The author states that the book was created to allow people of the future to find and unearth the capsule five thousand years later; this idea is described in answer choice A. While the author does tell us that the book lists the items in the time capsule, the passage does not state that the book tells how to use these items (answer choice B). Answer choice C is incorrect because the text from 1930s books and newspapers was put onto microfilm and buried inside of the capsule; it was not contained in the *Book of Record*. The book was also not meant for amusement (answer choice D). Answer choice A is the best answer.

4. Why did the Westinghouse engineers invent a new material for the creation of the time capsule?

   A. They needed to get rid of the company's steel and copper.
   B. They wanted to impress future peoples with their knowledge.
   C. They needed to protect the objects inside the capsule.
   D. They wanted to teach future peoples how to make Cupaloy.

This question asks you about a supporting detail from the passage. The passage tells you that Westinghouse engineers created a new material called Cupaloy that was as strong as steel and as resistant to corrosion as copper. Answer choice A is incorrect; they did not need to get rid of these materials. Answer choices B and D do not make sense because, in creating the time capsule, scientists understood that future people would be far more advanced and have much more knowledge than we have today. Answer choice C is best. The strong material was needed to protect the contents of the time capsule.


5. The author most likely included the information in the first paragraph of the passage to

   A   describe how the people of the past might have lived
   B   explain how archaeologists teach us about the past
   C   show readers how time capsules help people remember the past
   D   tell readers of the history of humankind up to the present century

This question asks you to decide what the main point of the first paragraph is. All of the answer choices are mentioned, but only one is the focus of the whole paragraph. The paragraph does talk about people of the past, but it does not talk about how they might have lived. They are only mentioned in reference to something else (answer choice A). Though the entire passage is about time capsules, this paragraph does not mention them until the final sentence, so answer choice C is incorrect. The paragraph talks about how people of the present learn about the history of humankind, but this is not the focus of the first paragraph. The paragraph is mostly about how we learn about people in the past, which is through the work of archaeologists. Answer choice B is correct.


6. Why did Westinghouse bury a second time capsule?

   A. to ensure that at least one would be found
   B. to include microfilm containing text from books
   C. to display it at the World's Fair in New York City
   D. to show that society had developed very quickly

You can find the answer to this question in the passage. Reread the paragraph discussing the second time capsule. Answer choice A is not correct, because this detail isn't mentioned in the passage. The first time capsule contained microfilm, so answer choice B is not the correct answer. Answer choice C is also not correct. The second time capsule wasn't created to display at the World's Fair. Answer choice D is the correct answer.

7. Why does the author most likely list the contents of both time capsules? Use information from the passage to support your answer.

This is a constructed-response question. You have to write out your answer to this question. Think about the items of each time capsule and why the author might have chosen to list those specific items. What was her purpose for including this information?

*One possible answer:*

*The author lists the contents of the time capsules for two reasons. First, she wants readers to know about the kinds of items that were chosen to represent life in the 1930s, as well as the types of items that might be included in a time capsule. Second, she is illustrating how much societal change took place between the burials of the first and the second time capsules. While the first contained a dollar bill, the second contained a credit card. A fountain pen was included in the first, and a ballpoint pen was included in the second. The first held a pair of eyeglasses, while the second held a pair of contact lenses. The author is trying to help readers to understand how much society had advanced over just twenty-seven years. She may also be encouraging readers to consider how much society could advance in 5,000 years, when the first time capsule is scheduled to be unearthed.*

# CHILE: THE LONG ROAD OF CHANGE

1   Chile is a nation on the western coast of South America. It is an unusually narrow country—less than 265 miles wide—but it is extremely long. Reaching almost 3,000 miles north to south, Chile extends along more than half of the continent. Along that distance, Chile varies from lush forests to farmlands to desolate deserts. On its eastern border are the Andes Mountains, and on the west is the Pacific Ocean. Chile is a land with many variations in its landscape. These variations mirror the many transitions Chile has undergone as a country.

## The First Chileans

2   The story of Chile began about 10,000 years ago when nomadic native groups began settling along South America's coasts. One group, known as the Mapuche, chose the coastal valleys as their home. These valleys had some fertile soil for planting, and hosted abundant game for hunting. Much of the area was hard to reach, and this kept the Mapuche safe from invasion for thousands of years. Even the mighty Incan empire failed to harness the Mapuche. Though the Inca spread across much of South America, they found the coastal land too harsh and isolated and could not establish a tight grip on it.

3   The Mapuche people remained safe from outsiders' interference until the 1500s, when explorers from Portugal and Spain stumbled across the land. The Spanish force arrived from neighboring Peru in search of gold and, five years later, decided to begin a colony on the Mapuche people's territory.

## The Name "Chile"

4   The colony came to be known as Chile, but the exact origin of that name is disputed. Some believe that it was derived from the name of a tribal chief who helped to ensure that the Inca did not overtake the land. Others think that Chile was named after a similar-looking area in Peru. Some less likely theories suggest that the country was named after the sound of its birds' songs. The best explanation for the name is that it comes from a Mapuche word meaning "where the land ends." The Mapuche, at first, did not know their neighbors and may have thought that theirs was the world's only civilization.

## Independence from Spain

5   Though Chile did not yield any great golden treasures for the Spanish, the colonists began establishing towns and farms. The native Mapuche, however, resented the Spanish invasion and, for the next hundred years, battled with the colonists. As generations passed, the various peoples of Chile came together and found a sense of pride in their nationality. Around 1810, Chileans began pushing for independence from Spain; after a long struggle, Chile declared its victory.

6   Independence did not improve the lives of most of its people. Wealthy landowners held great influence over the government while the native Mapuche people, along with poor farmers, suffered greatly. Through a series of treaties and wars, the

divisions among Chile's people became even more severe.

## Conflicts and Resolutions

7   By the 1920s, the people of Chile were demanding change. They elected reformist presidents who promised better lives for the people but consistently failed to provide them. Great dissatisfaction spread through Chile and several military groups within the country began attempting to take control. For decades, Chile was alternately run by military dictators and elected presidents.

8   When the Chilean government finally began to stabilize, the economy suddenly failed. Once again, fighting erupted. By the end of the battles, Chile's president had been overthrown and the country was controlled by a dictator, General Augusto Pinochet. Pinochet proved to be cruel and oppressive. By the end of his reign which lasted from 1973 to 1990, he had begun to give the people of Chile some rights—rights that they used to remove Pinochet from power.

9   Since then, Chile has entered a period of relative peace. Elected presidents have replaced dictators as the Chilean people struggle onward in their search for balance and prosperity. In January 2006, Michelle Bachelet, a pediatrician and a former minister of health and defense was elected president of Chile.

## An Enduring Culture

10   The Chileans have a long history and a strong, diverse culture. Over the centuries, their nation has been influenced by the Inca, Spanish colonists, and English and French traders. Each of these groups has left an impression on the people of Chile. For instance, one of Chile's traditional songs, the *tonada*, is a mixture of native and Spanish sounds and words.

11   Song is just one form of expression for which the people of Chile have become well known. Chile has also produced a number of celebrated writers, including Nobel Prize winners Pablo Neruda and Gabriela Mistral. Due to the accomplishments of Chile's wordsmiths, the country has nicknamed itself *país de poetas*—the "land of poets."

1. "When the Chilean government finally began to **stabilize**, the economy suddenly failed."

   What does the word **stabilize** mean?

   A. grow steady
   B. lose money
   C. treat people poorly
   D. gain world power

   This question asks about an unknown word from the passage. Look back to the passage and read the sentence which contains this word. The sentence talks about Chile's government finally improving when the economy suddenly breaks down. The paragraph and the sentences in it should give you clues about the meaning of the word. You can also look at the word itself; **stabilize** sounds like *stable*, which means "steady." Using this evidence, you can find that answer choice A is best.


2. What is the main problem that Chileans faced after winning their independence from Spain?

   A. They had a weak leader.
   B. They lacked education.
   C. They had poor soil for farming.
   D. They did not have much wealth.

   If you're not sure of the answer to this question, reread the information under the subheading, "Independence from Spain." Chile had many unsuccessful leaders (answer choice A), not just one weak leader. The passage doesn't mention whether or not Chileans were educated (answer choice B). While the author says in the beginning of the passage that Chile had poor soil (answer choice C), this wasn't the country's biggest problem after winning its independence. Answer choice D is the best answer; the author says that the people were poor and suffering.

3. What does this passage suggest about General Augusto Pinochet?

   A. He was a vicious leader.
   B. He lived with many regrets.
   C. He was always unsuccessful.
   D. He acted bravely in battle.

If you're not sure of the answer to this question, go back and reread what the passage says about Pinochet. The passage says that he was cruel and oppressive, so answer choice A is a good answer. The passage does not indicate that he was regretful (answer choice B). He was unsuccessful as a leader (answer choice C), but answer choice A is a better answer. Based on the information in the passage, we don't know whether or not he acted bravely in battle (answer choice D).


4. The author most likely wrote this passage in order to

   A. inform readers about a certain country
   B. compare one country with its neighbors
   C. persuade people to visit South America
   D. tell a story about Spanish explorers

Think about the passage you've just read. Why do you think that the author wrote this passage? What is the purpose of the passage? The author did mention Peru, one of Chile's neighbors, but he doesn't make any comparison (answer choice B). He does not attempt to draw new visitors to South America (answer choice C), and no part of this passage is written in a narrative, or "story," style (answer choice D). The author's main purpose in writing is to inform readers about a country, namely Chile. Answer choice A is best.


5. Why did Spanish explorers first travel to Chile?

   A. The coast of Chile was easy to reach by boat.
   B. Chile was the only country controlled by the Inca.
   C. They wanted access to Chile's rich farmland.
   D. They hoped to find golden treasures in Chile.

If you don't remember what caused the Spanish to move into Chile, you can look back to the passage. The passage does not mention boats (answer choice A), and says that Chile was not completely under Incan influence (answer choice B). Although the Spanish might have made good use of the rich farmland (answer choice C), that's not the reason they went to Chile. According to the passage, the reason is that the Spanish sought golden treasures (answer choice D).

6. Explain General Pinochet's effect on Chile, and why his removal from office led to further change. Use information from the passage to support your answer.

This question asks you to draw a conclusion about the effect a man had on Chile, and the effects of his removal from power. Since you have to answer this question with one or more written paragraphs, you should look back to the passage to refresh your memory and to gather information. Look for mention of Pinochet and of modern changes in Chile. Since this question has two parts, be sure to address them both thoroughly. First, tell how Pinochet changed life in Chile. Then, explain how Chile changed again once Pinochet was removed.

*One possible answer:*

*According to the passage, presidents and dictators competed for control of Chile during the 1900s. One dictator, General Augusto Pinochet, took charge. At first he was cruel to the people and took away their rights. This made the people upset and increased their desire for freedom. When Pinochet gave the people their rights back, they used their new powers to remove him from office. The author goes on to say that, since the people have gotten some power and have removed Pinochet, they have been electing presidents and moving toward a more balanced society.*

# JUMBO

1. Jumbo was an African bull elephant. He spent the first two decades of his life in captivity at England's London Zoo. He gave rides to thousands of children.

2. Jumbo was over twenty years old by the time he gained international attention, when he joined P.T. Barnum's circus in 1882. Jumbo came to symbolize the meaning of "big."

3. Jumbo was a small, scrawny baby elephant when he was captured in Central Africa. He was lovingly cared for, fed, groomed and trained by his keeper, Matthew Scott. He weighed an estimated seven tons and stood nearly twelve feet tall by the time Barnum sought to purchase him.

4. The London Zoological Society feared that the huge animal might one day become a danger to the public. Barnum's offer of $10,000 was readily accepted. However, English citizens from Queen Victoria to the man in the street protested the potential loss of what had become a national treasure.

5. Barnum delighted in the "Jumbo-mania" that raged between the two countries. He gained what he loved most—free publicity. Eventually, he refused to reconsider the deal. He transported Jumbo and Scott to America on board a huge freighter. The *Assyrian Monarch* sailed on a fifteen-day voyage across the Atlantic.

6. On Easter Sunday, 1882, Jumbo arrived at a dock in New York City. Thousands greeted him. Over the next three years, Jumbo was the focal point of the Barnum and Bailey Circus. He was viewed by an estimated twenty million people.

7. Jumbo died on September 15, 1885, in Canada. He was struck by a freight train. As with many things related to Barnum, stories vary about Jumbo's demise. Some say that he deliberately stood firm in the train's path. Others say that he had been attempting to protect a younger elephant named "Tom Thumb."

8. Barnum was determined to continue using Jumbo as an attraction. He contracted with a taxidermy firm to rebuild the giant elephant. His skin, weighing an estimated one thousand five hundred pounds, was stretched over a large wooden model. The "restored" Jumbo continued to appear with the circus for several years.

9. Eventually, Barnum donated Jumbo's skeleton of more than two thousand bones to the American Museum of Natural History in New York. He donated the mounted hide to Tufts University. It remained there until it was destroyed by fire in 1975.

10. Matthew Scott, Jumbo's longtime friend and trainer, was devastated by Jumbo's demise. He went on to care for small animals at the Barnum and Bailey Circus' winter headquarters in Bridgeport, Connecticut.

1. "Over the next three years, Jumbo was the **focal point** of the Barnum and Bailey Circus."

   What does the author mean when he writes that Jumbo was the **focal point** of the circus?

   A. Jumbo was the largest animal in the circus.
   B. Jumbo was the main attraction at the circus.
   C. Jumbo had been given many responsibilities.
   D. Jumbo had become a very famous animal.

2. What does this passage suggest about Matthew Scott?

   A. He was a caring trainer.
   B. He wasn't good at his job.
   C. He didn't like Mr. Barnum.
   D. He was a puzzling man.

3. The author most likely wrote this passage in order to

   A. encourage people to visit a circus.
   B. inform readers about an elephant's life.
   C. tell readers a story about famous animals.
   D. explain the development of a circus.

4. Why was Jumbo taken to New York City?

   A. He was going to give rides to children.
   B. He was dangerous to people.
   C. He had been struck by a freight train.
   D. He had been sold to a new owner.

5. Why do you think that Tufts University kept Jumbo's hide? Use information from the passage to support your answer.

# from "TARZAN OF THE APES" – Part I
## *by Edgar Rice Burroughs*

1. From early childhood he had used his hands to swing from branch to branch after the manner of his giant mother. As he grew older he spent hour upon hour daily speeding through the treetops with his brothers and sisters.

2. He could spring twenty feet across space at the dizzy heights of the forest top, and grasp with unerring precision, and without apparent jar, a limb waving wildly in the path of an approaching tornado.

3. He could drop twenty feet at a stretch from limb to limb in rapid descent to the ground, or he could gain the utmost pinnacle of the loftiest tropical giant with the ease and swiftness of a squirrel.

4. Though but ten years old he was fully as strong as the average man of thirty. He was far more agile than the most practiced athlete ever becomes. And day by day his strength was increasing.

5. His life among these fierce apes had been happy. His recollection held no other life, nor did he know that there existed within the universe aught else than his little forest and the wild jungle animals with which he was familiar.

6. He was nearly ten before he commenced to realize that a great difference existed between himself and his fellows. His little body, burned brown by exposure, suddenly caused him feelings of intense shame, for he realized that it was entirely hairless, like some low snake, or other reptile.

7. He attempted to obviate this by plastering himself from head to foot with mud, but this dried and fell off. Besides it felt so uncomfortable that he quickly decided that he preferred the shame to the discomfort.

8. In the higher land which his tribe frequented was a little lake. It was here that Tarzan first saw his face in the clear, still waters of its bosom.

9. It was on a sultry day of the dry season that he and one of his cousins had gone down to the bank to drink. As they leaned over, both little faces were mirrored on the placid pool; the fierce and terrible features of the ape beside those of the aristocratic scion of an old English house.

10. Tarzan was appalled. It had been bad enough to be hairless, but to own such a countenance! He wondered that the other apes could look at him at all.

11. That tiny slit of a mouth and those puny white teeth! How they looked beside the mighty lips and powerful fangs of his more fortunate brothers!

12   And the little pinched nose of his; so thin was it that it looked half starved. He turned red as he compared it with the beautiful broad nostrils of his companion. Such a generous nose!

13   Why it spread half across his face! "It certainly must be fine to be so handsome," thought poor little Tarzan.

14   But when he saw his own eyes; ah, that was the final blow—a brown spot, a gray circle and then blank whiteness! Frightful! Not even the snakes had such hideous eyes as he.


1. Why was Tarzan ashamed of his appearance?

   A. He had covered himself with mud.
   B. His ape friend made fun of his looks.
   C. His family members were unattractive.
   D. He looked so different from the apes.


2. What is this passage mostly about?

   A. how one boy escaped the jungle
   B. how apes and humans are alike
   C. a boy who lives among apes
   D. a boy who misses his family

3. What do Tarzan's ashamed feelings about himself suggest about how humans measure their own beauty and self-worth? Use information from the passage to support your answer.

# SEAT BELTS

1. Did you know that seat belts are the most effective means of reducing fatalities and serious injuries in a traffic crash? It's true. In fact, seat belts save over 10,000 lives in America every year.

2. The sad fact is that thousands of people still die in traffic crashes every year. When a vehicle is involved in a crash, passengers are still traveling at the vehicle's original speed at the moment of impact. When the vehicle finally comes to a complete stop, unbelted passengers slam into the steering wheel, windshield, or another part of the vehicle's interior. (Ouch!)

3. Seat belts are your best protection in a crash. They are designed so that the strongest areas of your body absorb the forces in a crash. Those are the areas along the bones of your hips, shoulders, and chest. The belts keep you in place so that your head, face, and chest are less likely to strike the windshield, dashboard, other vehicle interiors, or other passengers. They also keep you from being thrown out of a vehicle.

4. **The Top Four Reasons Why You Should Wear Your Seat Belt**

   - Seat belts can save your life in a crash.
   - Seat belts can reduce your risk of a serious injury in a crash.
   - Thousands of the people who die in car crashes each year might still be alive if they had been wearing their seat belts.
   - It's easy. It only takes three seconds.

5. What's the right way to wear your safety belt? The lap belt or lap portion of the lap/shoulder belt should be adjusted so that it is low and snug across the pelvis/lap area—never across the stomach. The shoulder belt should cross the chest and collarbone and be snug. The belt should never cross the front of the face or be placed behind your back.

6. The adult lap and shoulder belt will fit you properly when you can sit with your back against the vehicle seat back cushion, with knees bent over the vehicle seat edge and feet on the floor. So, to wear seat belts, you must be at least 4' 8" tall and weigh about eighty pounds.

7. If the lap and shoulder belt do not fit you right now, you should be using a belt-positioning booster seat! A booster seat raises your sitting height, which enables the lap and shoulder belt to fit you properly.

**How Seat Belts Can Stop You in a Crash**

8. One-tenth of a second after impact, the motor vehicle comes to a stop. The unbelted occupant slams into the car's interior. Immediately after the unbelted occupant stops

moving, his internal organs collide with each other and also with skeletal systems. To allow the occupant to come to a more gradual stop, all the stopping distance must be used. Holding you in your seat with a safety belt allows you to stop as the car is stopping, thereby enabling you to "ride down" the crash.

9     During a crash, safety belts distribute the forces of rapid deceleration over larger and stronger parts of the body such as the chest, hips, and shoulders. Additionally, the safety belt actually stretches slightly to slow down and to increase its stopping distance. The head, face, and chest are also less likely to strike the steering wheel, windshield, dashboard, or the car's interior frame.

10     People wearing safety belts are not thrown into another person or ejected from the vehicle. Also, the safety belt helps belted drivers maintain control of the car by keeping them in the driver's seat. This increases the chance of preventing a second crash.

### Seat Belts and Air Bags

11     You still must buckle your seat belt even if you're riding in a car with an air bag. Air bags can cause injuries or even death when people are too close at the time of deployment. Everyone should sit at least ten inches away from where the air bag is stored. Young children who are riding in child safety seats or older children who are riding in booster seats should ride in the back seat, furthest away from an air bag. In fact, children twelve years of age and under should always be properly buckled up in the back seat!

12     Front seat driver and passenger side air bags only work in frontal crashes, so if your car is hit on the side or rolls over, the air bag will not protect you—only your seat belt, when worn properly, can do that!

### Using Seat Belts with Child Safety Seats

13     Securing newborns and toddlers in child safety seats is known to reduce the chances of serious injury in a crash. Each child under the age of twelve should be buckled into her or his appropriate seat: the vehicle's back seat or a child safety seat in the back of the car. Newborns should be placed in rear-facing car seats in the back seat.

1. Which statement best describes the author's viewpoint about seat belts?

    A. Seat belts can harm children.
    B. Seat belts are difficult to use.
    C. Seat belts save many lives.
    D. Seat belts are uncomfortable.

2. According to the passage, what is the function of a booster seat?

   A. to protect kids from air bags
   B. to be used instead of a seat belt
   C. to make a seat belt fit properly
   D. to keep kids in the back seat

3. "Air bags can cause injuries or even death when people are too close at time of **deployment**."

   What does the word **deployment** mean?

   A. stopping work
   B. requiring repair
   C. going into action
   D. crashing into cars

4. According to the passage, which is more important for safety in crashes—a seat belt or an air bag? Use information from the passage to support your answer.

# from "THE CALL OF THE WILD"
## *by Jack London*

1. Buck had accepted the rope with quiet dignity. To be sure, it was an unwonted performance but he had learned to trust in men he knew, and to give them credit for a wisdom that outreached his own. But when the ends of the rope were placed in the stranger's hands, he growled menacingly. He had merely intimated his displeasure, in his pride believing that to intimate was to command. But to his surprise the rope tightened around his neck, shutting off his breath. In a quick rage he sprang at the man, who met him halfway, grappled him close by the throat, and with a deft twist threw him over on his back. Then the rope tightened mercilessly, while Buck struggled in a fury, his tongue lolling out of his mouth and his great chest panting futilely. Never in all his life had he been so vilely treated, and never in all his life had he been so angry. But his strength ebbed, his eyes glazed, and he knew nothing when the train was flagged and the two men threw him into the baggage car.

2. The next he knew, he was dimly aware that his tongue was hurting and that he was being jolted along in some kind of a conveyance. The hoarse shriek of a locomotive whistling a crossing told him where he was. He had traveled too often with the Judge not to know the sensation of riding in a baggage car. He opened his eyes, and into them came the unbridled anger of a kidnapped king. The man sprang for his throat, but Buck was too quick for him. His jaws closed on the hand, nor did they relax till his senses were choked out of him once more.

3. "Yep, has fits," the man said, hiding his mangled hand from the baggage man, who had been attracted by the sounds of struggle. "I'm taking him up for the boss to 'Frisco. A crack dog doctor there thinks that he can cure him."

4. Concerning that night's ride, the man spoke most eloquently for himself, in a little shed back of a saloon on the San Francisco waterfront.

5. "All I get is fifty for it," he grumbled, "and I wouldn't do it over for a thousand, cold cash."

6. His hand was wrapped in a bloody handkerchief, and the right trouser leg was ripped from knee to ankle.

7. "How much did the other mug get?" the saloon-keeper demanded.

8. "A hundred," was the reply. "Wouldn't take a sou less, so help me."

9. "That makes a hundred and fifty," the saloon-keeper calculated, "and he's worth it, or I'm a squarehead."

10. The kidnapper undid the bloody wrappings and looked at his lacerated hand. "If I don't get hydrophobia—"

11   "It'll be because you was born to hang," laughed the saloon-keeper. "Here, lend me a hand before you pull your freight," he added.

12   Dazed, suffering intolerable pain from throat and tongue, with the life half throttled out of him, Buck attempted to face his tormentors. But he was thrown down and choked repeatedly, till they succeeded in filing the heavy brass collar from off his neck. Then the rope was removed, and he was flung into a cage-like crate.

1. "In a quick rage he sprang at the man, who met him halfway, grappled him close by the throat, and with a **deft** twist threw him over on his back."

   What does the word **deft** mean?

   A. skillful
   B. quick
   C. tight
   D. gentle

2. Why does the man put a rope around Buck's neck?

   A. because the man hates dogs
   B. because Buck is a wild dog
   C. because the man wants to capture Buck
   D. because the man is afraid to go near Buck

3. Which word best describes how Buck feels when he wakes up in the baggage car?

   A. furious
   B. scared
   C. confused
   D. obedient

4. "Dazed, suffering **intolerable** pain from throat and tongue, with the life half throttled out of him, Buck attempted to face his tormentors."

   The information in this sentence suggests that the word **intolerable** means

   A. wonderful
   B. strange
   C. unbearable
   D. imagined

5. Which statement best shows that Buck was determined?

   A. " . . . To be sure, it was an unwonted performance but he had learned to trust in men he knew . . . "
   B. "But to his surprise the rope tightened around his neck, shutting off his breath."
   C. " . . . with the life half throttled out of him, Buck attempted to face his tormentors."
   D. "Then the rope was removed, and he was flung into a cage-like crate."


6. Think about the characters and events in this passage. Around which period in history do you think this story takes place? Use information from the passage to support your answer.

# COMMUNICATION

1. Ever hear the story of the couple who, on the eve of their fiftieth anniversary, sat down for a snack? With makings for a sandwich before him, the husband reached into a new bag of bread and handed his wife the heel. She then burst out, "For fifty years you have been giving me the heel. I won't take it anymore! When will you think of me for a change?" "But, Honey," he replied with shock, "I gave you my favorite part!"

2. Communication snafus happen in the best of relationships. Sometimes the solution is as simple as asking questions to ensure that you have understood your partner accurately.

3. There are many ways of communicating in a relationship. Some will be productive and move each of you to a higher level of understanding about each other. Some will not. Learning how to communicate effectively is a skill that takes practice. It is important to recognize poor communication styles. Once you recognize them you can begin to repair them.

4. A passive communication style is one in which someone is not honestly identifying his or her feelings. This is the "martyr syndrome." The passive communicator risks being treated like a doormat. Another style is an aggressive style of communication. This individual tries to communicate through intimidation. Unfortunately, this style of communication is also ineffective. It usually makes people defensive. Another dysfunctional style of communication is a passive-aggressive style. This person presents as passive or benign on the surface. However, in hidden, underhanded ways she or he sets out to undermine or diminish another individual.

5. Communication is not a contest. It's not like a debate, where there is one winner. Rather, the best result is a "win-win" situation where both parties achieve a better understanding of the other's feelings. Communication is a skill that can be learned. A key component is active listening.

6. An effective listener doesn't force the speaker to do all the work. He or she enters into the process. Be patient with pauses. Don't rush a speaker who seems to be blocked momentarily. Rather, feed back a few of the last words spoken or feelings expressed. Keep an open mind. Before disagreeing, make sure that you've fully comprehended what was said. Both partners get to practice expressing their own feelings in a given situation, allowing the other adequate opportunity to present ideas, too. Ask for clarification if any point is confusing. Try not to be defensive. Rather than preparing a retort, really listen to what the other person is saying. Acknowledge feelings, rather than attributing them to the other party.

7. Expressing what you feel and need to a partner is very important. So much of the time, we expect our partner to "know what we need" without having to say it. This is an unreasonable expectation. It often leads to serious disappointments and feelings of inadequacy.

- I feel . . .
- I need for you to . . .
- I am willing to . . .
- What do you need from me?

8   Practicing this exchange can lead to a better understanding of what each of you is really expecting and hoping for in the relationship.

1. The author most likely included the anecdote about the elderly couple in paragraph 1 to

   A. get the readers' attention
   B. make readers aware of a problem
   C. teach an important lesson
   D. reach an important conclusion

2. What is the most likely reason for including the first two paragraphs?

   A. to show how communication can be improved
   B. to show how lack of communication can lead to problems
   C. to show what is most important when speaking with a partner
   D. to show what people can do to be better listeners

3. "Communication **snafus** like this one happen in even the best of relationships."

   What does the word **snafus** mean?

   A. examples
   B. blunders
   C. types
   D. insults

4. According to the passage, which of the following is a trait of a good listener?

    A. helping the speaker finish sentences
    B. making sure that the message has been understood
    C. letting the speaker do all of the work
    D. repeating the last words the speaker said

5. The author portrays communication as being

    A. learned with regular practice
    B. disappointing for speakers
    C. a contest between ideas
    D. a skill that everyone naturally has

6. Briefly explain two examples of good communication and two examples of bad communication. Use information from the passage to support your answer.

# RALPH NADER

1. Ralph Nader was born in 1934 in the small factory town of Winsted, Connecticut. His parents were proud Lebanese immigrants. His father, Nathra Nader, ran the Highland Arms Restaurant in town. He engaged his customers in spirited debate about public affairs.

2. As a child, Ralph was studious, bright, and intense. His parents challenged and inspired their four children—two sons and two daughters—to think for themselves, to have opinions, and to stand up for what they believed was right. They even took their children to town government meetings to learn what it truly meant when one person spoke out.

3. Ralph played with David Halberstam, the future journalist, when they were both young boys. He also read back issues of the *Congressional Record*. By the age of fourteen, he had read the early "muckrakers." They inspired his thinking about the distribution of power in American society. He graduated *magna cum laude* from Princeton in 1955. In 1958, he graduated from Harvard Law School.

4. It was at Harvard that Ralph first explored an unorthodox legal topic: the engineering design of automobiles. He was concerned about safety. He knew that there were five million automobile accidents reported every year. These accidents caused nearly 40,000 fatalities, 110,000 permanent disabilities, and 1.5 million injuries annually.

5. His research resulted in an April 1959 article, published in *The Nation*. It was called "The Safe Car You Can't Buy." In this article, Ralph declared, "Detroit is designing automobiles for style, cost and performance. Cars are not designed for safety."

6. In 1963, Ralph was an unknown twenty-nine-year-old attorney. He decided to change his life. He abandoned a law practice in Hartford, Connecticut. He hitchhiked to Washington, D.C. There he began a long life of professional citizenship.

7. "I had one suitcase," he recalled. "I stayed in the YMCA. Walked across a little street and had a hot dog, my last." A few years later, he would expose the repulsive ingredients that go into hot dogs.

8. Ralph took a job as a consultant to the U.S. Department of Labor. He worked for Assistant Secretary of Labor Daniel Patrick Moynihan. He moonlighted as a freelance writer for *The Nation*. He also wrote for *The Christian Science Monitor*. He acted as an unpaid adviser to a Senate subcommittee. The subcommittee was exploring the role that the federal government might play in auto safety.

9. In 1965, armed with a wealth of research and a passion for the topic, Ralph targeted General Motors (GM) and the American auto industry. His bestselling book was called *Unsafe at Any Speed: The Designed-In Dangers of the American Automobile*. Using all sorts of immoral and underhanded tactics, GM attempted to discredit him.

He then sued them for invasion of privacy. This landmark case forced the president of GM to go before a Senate committee. He had to admit that GM had behaved improperly. The money Ralph received when the case was settled was the most ever received for a lawsuit of this type. A series of safety laws was passed in 1966. These laws forced the auto industry to make drastic design changes so that motor vehicles would be safer. With the money Ralph had won in the settlement, he launched the modern consumer movement.

10   Ralph Nader continues to speak out today, calling attention to the situations and the practices that he and his "Nader's Raiders" believe to be questionable or wrong. He has run three times for the office of president of the United States, once in 1996, again in 2000, and then in 2004. His campaigns have brought significant attention to his message and to his political party at the time, the Green Party. Ralph Nader has never forgotten his humble roots, however, as he describes them in his memoir, *The Seventeen Traditions*, published in January 2007.

1. The author most likely wrote this passage in order to

   A. show how cars have become safer over the years
   B. persuade readers to give up hot dogs and hamburgers
   C. describe what it is like to attend Harvard Law School
   D. inform readers about a man who has helped consumers

2. According to the passage, how did Ralph Nader make enough money to start an organization?

   A. He had a law practice.
   B. He wrote a best-selling book.
   C. He settled a lawsuit.
   D. He advised a Senate committee.

3. What became Ralph Nader's principal focus when he was a young man?

   A. auto safety
   B. practicing law
   C. impressing others
   D. making money

4. Which statement is supported by the passage?
   A. Ralph Nader hated going to his classes.
   B. Ralph Nader helped the car companies.
   C. Ralph Nader wanted to help people.
   D. Ralph Nader dreamed of being rich.

5. What do you think the modern consumer movement involves? Use information from the passage to support your answer.

# from "TARZAN OF THE APES" – Part II
## *by Edgar Rice Burroughs*

1. He did not hear the parting of the tall grass behind him as a great body pushed itself stealthily through the jungle. Nor did his companion, the ape, hear either, for he was drinking. The noise of his sucking lips and gurgles of satisfaction drowned the quiet approach of the intruder.

2. Not thirty paces behind the two she crouched—Sabor, the huge lioness—lashing her tail. Cautiously she moved a great padded paw forward, noiselessly placing it before she lifted the next. Thus she advanced; her belly low, almost touching the surface of the ground—a great cat preparing to spring upon its prey.

3. Now she was within ten feet of the two unsuspecting little playfellows. Carefully she drew her hind feet well up beneath her body, the great muscles rolling under the beautiful skin. So low she was crouching now that she seemed flattened to the earth except for the upward bend of the glossy back as it gathered for the spring. No longer the tail lashed. Quiet and straight behind her it lay.

4. An instant she paused thus, as though turned to stone, and then, with an awful scream, she sprang.

5. Sabor, the lioness, was a wise hunter. To one less wise the wild alarm of her fierce cry as she sprang would have seemed a foolish thing, for could she not more surely have fallen upon her victims had she but quietly leaped without that loud shriek?

6. But Sabor knew well the wondrous quickness of the jungle folk and their almost unbelievable powers of hearing. To them the sudden scraping of one blade of grass across another was as effectual a warning as her loudest cry. Sabor knew that she could not make that mighty leap without a little noise.

7. Her wild scream was not a warning. It was voiced to freeze her poor victims in a paralysis of terror for the tiny fraction of an instant which would suffice for her mighty claws to sink into their soft flesh and hold them beyond hope of escape.

8. So far as the ape was concerned, Sabor reasoned correctly. The little fellow crouched trembling just an instant, but that instant was quite long enough to prove his undoing.

9. Not so, however, with Tarzan, the man-child. His life amidst the dangers of the jungle had taught him to meet emergencies with self-confidence, and his higher intelligence resulted in a quickness of mental action far beyond the powers of the apes.

10. So the scream of Sabor, the lioness, galvanized the brain and muscles of little Tarzan into instant action.

11  Before him lay the deep waters of the little lake, behind him certain death; a cruel death beneath tearing claws and rending fangs.

1. In the first paragraph, the author interests readers by describing

    A. how a lion in the jungle pounces
    B. an unknown danger approaching
    C. a calm scene with an ape drinking
    D. the tall grass that can hide dangers

2. Why does Sabor unleash a fierce cry before pouncing on her victims?

    A. She wants to warn them.
    B. She wants to chase them.
    C. She wants to scare them.
    D. She wants to name them.

3. Why is Tarzan able to get away?

    A. He quickly moves into action.
    B. He is able to outrun Sabor.
    C. He is very close to the lake.
    D. He can hear Sabor approach.

4. "So the scream of Sabor, the lioness, **galvanized** the brain and muscles of little Tarzan into instant action."

    What does the word **galvanized** mean?

    A. stimulated
    B. undid
    C. terrified
    D. created

5. The author skillfully makes it possible for readers to visualize the scene at the edge of the lake where Tarzan and the small ape have paused for a drink. Although the shrill cry of the lioness had succeeded in freezing the ape in fear, it had just the opposite effect on Tarzan who immediately went into action. Explain how Tarzan knew just what to do at a time like this, and then tell how he reacted to Sabor's attack.

# KRISTINE LILLY

1   Kristine Marie Lilly was born in New York City on July 22, 1971. She grew up in Wilton, Connecticut. At a young age, she quickly became an excellent soccer player. When she was a student at Wilton High School, Kristine's team won state soccer titles during her freshman, sophomore, and senior years. She served as team captain as a junior and senior.

2   While still a high school student, Kristine debuted for the national women's soccer team. Kristine's debut performance was during the sixteenth match ever played by the U.S. Women's team. The date was August 3, 1987. At the age of 16 years and 12 days, she was the second youngest player ever to don a U.S. jersey. Mia Hamm, her teammate, was the youngest.

3   Kristine attended the University of North Carolina (UNC), where she was a four-time first selection All-American. She was twice named the "Most Valuable Player" (MVP) of the NCAA Championship. She helped to lead UNC to four NCAA championships from 1989 to 1992. Kristine completed her collegiate career with 78 goals and 41 assists.

4   Kristine's junior year in college proved to be very rewarding. She won the 1991 Hermann Trophy as the best female college soccer player in America. She was also a finalist for the Broderick Award as the outstanding female athlete in all of college sports. She was the second-leading scorer in the nation with fifteen goals and four assists. Mia Hamm was first. In December of 1993, Kristine graduated from UNC with a degree in communications. Just one year later, her UNC number (15) was retired.

5   After college, Kristine Lilly went on to help the USA win two Women's World Cups and numerous international tournaments. She scored three pivotal goals during the 1996 Olympic games, earning the team the gold medal. In 1999, Kristine led the National Team with twenty goals and played a crucial role in the World Cup final game against China. She cleared a Chinese shot off the goal line with her head in sudden death overtime. She also nailed the third penalty kick resulting in a U.S. win, 5–4. Kristine was named MVP of the U.S. Women's Cup in 1999. She was an All-Tournament selection in 1995, 1996, and 1997.

6   On January 18, 2006, Kristine earned her 300th cap for the U.S. Women's team in a game against Norway. A cap is a recognition earned by a player for each appearance in an international game for his or her country. She is the first player in soccer history, man or woman, to reach that milestone. She is tied with Michelle Akers for second place on the team's all-time goal scoring list with 105.

7   Kristine has played for nearly twenty years on the national team. The left-footed, left-sided mid-fielder has established herself as one of the top players in the world. Her hometown of Wilton, Connecticut, dedicated a day to her and honored her with a parade after she won the gold medal. A road sign entering her town reads,

"Welcome to Wilton: Hometown of Olympic Gold Medalist Kristine Lilly." Kristine runs the Kristine Lilly Soccer Academy every summer in Wilton. Following the Women's World Cup victory, the Wilton High School soccer field was named after her.

1. What is this passage mostly about?

    A. the final match of a the Women's World Cup
    B. an interesting and talented soccer player
    C. how to start a soccer league in your school
    D. the women of the National Soccer Team

2. "In 1999, Kristine led the National Team with 20 goals and played a **crucial** role in the World Cup final game against China."

    The information in this sentence suggests that the word **crucial** means

    A. key
    B. painful
    C. honorary
    D. colorful

3. Which award did Kristine Lilly win in 1991?

    A. U.S. Women's Cup MVP
    B. Broderick Award
    C. Hermann Trophy
    D. Wilton High School title

4. The "Kristine Lilly" passage is most similar to

    A. a list of regulations
    B. a newspaper article
    C. a local sports report
    D. an historical fiction

# SENGBE PIEH (CINQUE): CAPTURE, REVOLT, AND RECAPTURE

## THE CAPTURE

1   Sengbe Pieh was born about 1813. He was the son of a local chief. He was born in the town of Mani in Upper Mende country. It was ten days' march from the Atlantic coast. Sengbe became a farmer and got married; he and his wife had a son and two daughters.

2   One day in late January 1839, he was going to his field. He was captured in a surprise attack by four men. He was taken to a nearby village to a man called Mayagilalo. After three days, Mayagilalo gave Sengbe over to a local king, King Siaka, in payment of a debt. After staying in Siaka's town for a month, Sengbe was marched to Lomboko, a notorious slave-trading island. He was sold to the richest slaver there, the Spaniard Pedro Blanco, whose activities had helped to make King Siaka wealthy as well.

3   At Lomboko, Sengbe was imprisoned with other slaves. More slaves joined them for the two months they were there. They all were waiting to be transported across the Atlantic. Most of the captives came from Mende country. Some, who did not speak Mende, learned the language during their forced journey through Mende country to the coast. Most were farmers. Others were hunters and blacksmiths. This is surprising because all over West Africa, blacksmiths held a sacred place in society and could neither be enslaved nor killed even during war.

4   All these people were shipped from Lomboko in March aboard the schooner *Tecora*, which arrived at Havana in the Spanish colony of Cuba in June. At a slave auction following an advertisement, Jose Ruiz, a Spanish plantation owner, bought Sengbe and forty-eight others for $450 each to work on his sugar plantation at Puerto Principe, another Cuban port three hundred miles from Havana. Pedro Montez, another Spaniard bound for the same port, bought three girls and a boy.

5   On June 26th, the fifty-three Africans were herded on board an American-built schooner. It had originally been called *Friendship*, but was changed to the Spanish *La Amistad* when the vessel changed ownership and was registered as a Spanish subject.

## THE REVOLT

6   The trip to Puerto Principe usually took three days, but the winds were adverse. Three days out at sea, on June 30th, Sengbe used a loose spike that he had removed from the deck to unshackle himself and his fellow slaves. They had been whipped and maltreated and, at one point, made to believe that they would be killed for supper on arrival. Sengbe armed himself and the others with cane knives found in the cargo hold. He then led them on deck, where they killed Captain Ferrer and the cook Celestino and wounded the Spaniard Montez. Sengbe spared Montez's life along

with those of Ruiz and Antonio, the cabin boy. The mutineers lost two of their own party, killed by Captain Ferrer. Two white seamen managed to escape from the *Amistad* in a small boat.

7   Sengbe then ordered the Spaniards to sail in the direction of the rising of the sun, or eastward towards Africa. At night, however, Montez, who had some experience as a sailor, navigated by the stars and sailed westward. He was hoping to remain in Cuban waters. Nevertheless, a gale drove the ship northeasterly along the United States coastline. The schooner followed a zigzag course for two months, during which time eight more slaves died of thirst and exposure. Sengbe held command the whole time, forcing the others to conserve food and water, and allotting a full ration only to the four children. He took the smallest portion for himself.

**RECAPTURE**

8   The *Amistad* drifted off Long Island, New York, in late August 1839. Sengbe and others went ashore to trade for food and supplies and to negotiate with local seamen to take them back to Africa. News soon got around about a mysterious ship in the neighborhood with her "sails nearly all blown to pieces." It was the "long, low, black schooner," the story of which had been appearing in newspapers in previous weeks as the ship cruised in a northeastern direction along the U.S. coastline. Reports said that Cuban slaves had revolted and killed the crew of a Spanish ship and were roaming the Atlantic as buccaneers.

9   On August 26th, the United States survey brig *Washington* sighted the battered schooner near Culloden Point on the eastern tip of Long Island. The United States Navy and the Customs Service had previously issued orders for the capture of the ship.

10  When the *Amistad* was captured, a reporter from the *New York Sun* witnessed Sengbe's defiance of and repeated attempts to escape from his captors. Sengbe jumped overboard. He had to be dragged back onto the ship. He urged his fellow slaves to fight against hopeless odds. He was taken away to the American vessel and separated from his men. He made such a violent protest that the naval officers allowed him to remain on the *Washington*'s deck, where he stood and stared fixedly at the *Amistad* throughout the night.

1.  Which statement best represents the main problem Sengbe Pieh faced in the passage?

    A. His friends were arrested by the navy.
    B. He had been hurt and lost in another country.
    C. His ship was lost in the Atlantic Ocean.
    D. He had been captured and forced into slavery.

2. "The trip to Puerto Principe usually took three days, but the winds were **adverse**."

   What does the word **adverse** mean?

   A. refreshing
   B. unfavorable
   C. frightening
   D. nonexistent

3. Which statement best describes the author's viewpoint toward Sengbe Pieh?

   A. He was a noble and heroic figure.
   B. He was a poor sailor and a bad leader.
   C. He thought that he had returned to Africa.
   D. He thought that King Siaka should have freed him.

4. Which of these is most likely to occur?

   A. Sengbe Pieh will be set free.
   B. Sengbe Pieh will try to escape.
   C. The navy will hire Sengbe Pieh.
   D. The ship will finally sink.

5. Sengbe Pieh was a mysterious and thought-provoking figure. His struggle greatly affected people in the United States and it continues to do so even today; some think that he symbolized fear and death, and others believe that he is a symbol of freedom. Choose which you think Sengbe Pieh best symbolizes, explain your choice, and use information from the passage to support your response.

# THE COMPLICATED LIFE OF A PATUXENT WHOOPER EGG

1. In nature, whooping cranes usually mate, establish territory, build a nest, and then lay two eggs. If everything goes right, they will raise one chick. Life for the Patuxent whooper cranes—and for the people who care for them—is more complicated.

2. At the U.S. Geological Survey's Patuxent Wildlife Research Center, whoopers usually mate, establish territory in their pen, build a nest, and then lay two eggs, which is called a "clutch." However, the birds don't get to keep these eggs. After they lay the second egg, we remove the clutch. Why? Because removing the clutch after it has been laid causes the cranes to lay again in about ten days. By taking the eggs away, we can increase production by three or four times. So instead of only laying two eggs and raising at the most one chick, as they would in the wild, Patuxent's whoopers may lay six or eight eggs each year. The whoopers are usually allowed to incubate their last egg and raise the chick themselves.

3. What happens to all the other eggs? Whooper eggs do best if incubated by cranes instead of by mechanical incubators, at least in the early stages. Every time we remove an egg, we take it to the propagation building, carrying it in a rigid suitcase redesigned to be a portable incubator. The eggs are handled carefully, since jostling them and temperature extremes can kill a fragile embryo. At the propagation building, the eggs are weighed, measured, and examined to make sure that they are not cracked or have weak shells. (Eggs with cracks or thin shells will have to receive special care if we hope to hatch a chick from them.)

4. We give each egg an identification number based on the parent's pen location and the order in which the egg was laid. This number is written directly on the egg's shell with a lab marker. After this is done, we bring the egg back to the crane pens and place it under an incubating sandhill crane for the next ten days.

5. Patuxent maintains a flock of Florida and greater sandhill cranes, both for incubating whooper eggs and for providing non-endangered birds to use in studies. Pairs of sandhill cranes are rated, based on previous years' breeding experience, on their incubation and parenting skills. Only the highest-rated pairs are trusted with whooper eggs. Detailed charts are kept on each pair's breeding schedule—when they laid their own eggs and how long they've been incubating—so that the birds will be ready when we give them a whooper egg.

6. The surrogate sandhills will incubate the whooper egg for ten days. Both the male and the female will take turns caring for it. After ten days, we'll remove it, take it back to the propagation building, and weigh and examine it again to see if it's fertile. Weighing it also tells us if the egg has lost too much weight. A fertile egg is a living thing. All fertile eggs lose weight as the chick inside grows and uses up the egg's material. However, excessive weight loss indicates that the egg is dehydrating too quickly. We often remedy problems like this, since the egg weight is critical.

7  If the egg is fertile and healthy, flock manager Jane will check the charts to decide which pair of sandhills would be best to incubate the egg for the next ten days. After those twenty days, the whooper egg will be brought in again to make sure that it is developing normally. At twenty days, it is safe to place the egg in a mechanical incubator for the last ten days of incubation.

8  Managing the care of whooper eggs means knowing what stage of incubation they're at, what condition they're in and, most importantly, where they are. At the height of the breeding season, there might be over 50 whooper eggs and over 100 sandhill eggs to keep track of. Since all crane eggs look similar, proper identification of each individual egg and careful record-keeping is critical. Even if we're in a hurry—and in the breeding season, we're always in a hurry—paperwork must be done precisely and on time.

1. The author most likely wrote this passage in order to
    A. encourage readers to learn more about how eggs hatch
    B. tell readers about the dangers that whooper cranes face
    C. inform readers about caring for whooper crane eggs
    D. give readers information about raising whooper cranes

2. At the research center, how are Patuxent whooper crane eggs first incubated?
    A. by a mechanical incubator
    B. by Patuxent whooper crane parents
    C. by pairs of sandhill cranes
    D. by a propagation building

3. What technique does the author use to communicate the information about whooper crane eggs?
    A. giving an account of those who work with whooper crane eggs
    B. giving questions and answers from people interested in bird watching
    C. quoting from scientists who study the eggs of many animals
    D. reporting interviews with scientists who study birds of all kinds

4. The jobs of the people who work with Patuxent whooping crane eggs are portrayed by the author as being

   A. funny and surprising
   B. difficult yet rewarding
   C. dangerous and scary
   D. tiresome yet peaceful

5. Identify and explain at least two of the most important elements of proper whooper crane egg care. Use details from the passage to support your answer.

# from "A FANCY OF HERS" – Part I
## *by Horatio Alger*

1   The new school teacher was sitting at the window in her room, supper being over, when the landlady came up to inform her that Squire Hadley had called to see her.

2   "He is the chairman of the School Committee, isn't he?" asked the stranger.

3   "Yes, miss."

4   "Then will you be kind enough to tell him that I will be down directly?"

5   Squire Hadley was sitting in a rocking chair in the stiff hotel parlor, when Miss Frost entered, and said composedly, "Mr. Hadley, I believe?"

6   She exhibited more self-possession than might have been expected of one in her position, in the presence of official importance. There was not the slightest trace of nervousness in her manner, though she was aware that the portly person before her was to examine into her qualifications for the post she sought.

7   "I apprehend," said Squire Hadley, in a tone of dignity which he always put on when he addressed teachers, "I apprehend that you are Miss Mabel Frost."

8   "You are quite right, sir. I apprehend," she added, with a slight smile, "that you are the chairman of the School Committee."

9   "You apprehend correctly, Miss Frost. It affords me great pleasure to welcome you to Granville."

10  "You are very kind," said Mabel Frost demurely.

11  "It is a responsible, office—ahem!—that of instructor of youth," said the Squire, with labored gravity.

12  "I hope I appreciate it."

13  "Have you ever—ahem!—taught before?

14  "This will be my first school."

15  "This—ahem!—is against you, but I trust you may succeed."

16  "I trust so, sir."

17  "You will have to pass an examination in the studies you are to teach—before ME," said the Squire.

18 "I hope you may find me competent," said Mabel modestly,

19 "I hope so, Miss Frost; my examination will be searching. I feel it my duty to the town to be very strict."

20 "Would you like to examine me now, Mr. Hadley?"

21 "No," said the Squire hastily, "no, no—I haven't my papers with me. I will trouble you to come to my house tomorrow morning, at nine o'clock, if convenient."

22 "Certainly, sir. May I ask where your house is?"

23 "My boy shall call for you in the morning."

24 "Thank you."

25 Mabel spoke as if this terminated the colloquy, but Squire Hadley had something more to say.

26 "I think we have said nothing about your wages, Miss Frost," he remarked.

27 "You can pay me whatever is usual," said Mabel, with apparent indifference.

28 "We have usually paid seven dollars a week."

29 "That will be quite satisfactory, sir."

30 Soon after Squire Hadley had left the hotel Mabel Frost went slowly up to her room.

31 "So I am to earn seven dollars a week," she said to herself. "This is wealth indeed!"


1. Which word best describes Squire Hadley?
    A. lazy
    B. dignified
    C. friendly
    D. informal

2. "There was not the slightest trace of nervousness in her manner, though she was aware that the **portly** person before her was to examine into her qualifications for the post she sought."

   What does the word **portly** mean?
   - A. nervous
   - B. hiding
   - C. stout
   - D. conceited

3. Mabel's reaction to Squire Hadley suggests that she finds the whole encounter
   - A. annoying.
   - B. amusing.
   - C. nerve-wracking.
   - D. strange.

# from "A FANCY OF HERS" – Part II
## *by Horatio Alger*

1. In the evening Allan Thorpe called and invited Mabel to go out for a walk. It was a beautiful moonlight night. They walked slowly to the pond, which was not far away, and sat down on a rustic seat beneath a wide spreading oak. They had been talking on various things for some time, when a sudden silence came upon both. It was at length broken by the young artist.

2. "I hope you will forgive me for bringing you here," he said.

3. "Why should you want forgiveness?" she asked, very much surprised.

4. "Because I brought you here with a special object in view. Rebuke me if you will, but—Mabel, I love you."

5. She did not seem much surprised.

6. "How long has it been so?" she asked in a low voice.

7. "I began to love you," he answered, "when I first saw you at the artists' reception. But you were so far removed from me that I did not dare to avow it, even to myself. You were a rich social queen, and I was a poor man. I should never have dared to tell you all this if you had not lost your wealth."

8. "Does this make me any more worthy?" asked Mabel, smiling.

9. "It has brought you nearer to me. When I saw how bravely you met adverse fortune; when I saw a girl brought up to every luxury, as you were, quietly devoting herself to teaching a village school, I rejoiced. I admired you more than ever, and I resolved to win you if possible. Can you give me a hope, Mabel?"

10. He bent over her with a look of tender affection in his manly face.

11. "I won't keep you in suspense, Allan," she said with an answering look. "I have not known you long but long enough to trust my future in your hands."

12. After a while Allan Thorpe began to discuss his plans and hopes for the future.

13. "I am beginning to be successful," he said. "I can, even now, support you in a modest way, and with health I feel assured of a larger—I hope a much larger—income in time. I can relieve you from teaching at once."

14. Mabel smiled.

15. "But suppose I do not consider it a burden. Suppose I like it."

16   "Then you can teach me."

17   "It might become monotonous to have only one pupil."

18   "I hope not," said Allan earnestly.

19   When he pressed her to name an early day for their marriage, Mabel said: "Before we go any further, I have a confession to make. I hope it won't be disagreeable to you."

20   He silently inclined his head to listen.

21   "Who told you I had lost my property?" she asked.

22   "No one. I inferred it from finding you here, teaching a village school for seven dollars a week," replied Allan.

23   "What! Have you inquired my income so exactly? I fear you are mercenary."

24   "I can remember the time—not so long since, either—when I earned less than that by my art. But, Mabel, what do you mean by your questions? Of course you have lost your property."

25   "Then my banker has failed to inform me of it. No, Allan, I am no poorer than I ever was."

26   "Why, then, did you become a teacher?" asked Allan Thorpe, bewildered.

27   "Because I wished to be of some service to my kind; because I was tired of the hollow frivolity of the fashionable world. I don't regret my experiment. I never expected to be so richly rewarded."

28   "And you, as rich as ever, bestow your hand on a poor artist?" he exclaimed almost incredulously.

29   "Unless the poor artist withdraws his offer," she answered with a smile.


1.  Why did Allan Thorpe bring Mabel to the pond?

    A. to see the moonlight
    B. to show her some art
    C. to discuss her wealth
    D. to declare his love

2. Why does Allan Thorpe think that Mabel has lost her fortune?

   A. She is interested in marrying him.
   B. She doesn't tell him about her banker.
   C. She is a teacher in the village.
   D. She doesn't like social events.

3. Which word best describes Allan Thorpe?

   A. relaxed
   B. rowdy
   C. wealthy
   D. humble

4. Mabel said that she had found something lacking in her previous life. Identify and explain one thing that Mabel most likely did not like about her life before. Then identify and explain two ways in which Mabel was "richly rewarded," as she mentions in paragraph 27.

# from "PETER PAN"
## by J.M. Barrie

1. Mrs. Darling loved to have everything just so, and Mr. Darling had a passion for being exactly like his neighbours; so, of course, they had a nurse. As they were poor, owing to the amount of milk the children drank, this nurse was a prim Newfoundland dog, called Nana, who had belonged to no one in particular until the Darlings engaged her. She had always thought children important, however. The Darlings had become acquainted with her in Kensington Gardens, where she spent most of her spare time peeping into perambulators, and was much hated by careless nursemaids, whom she followed to their homes and complained of to their mistresses.

2. She proved to be quite a treasure of a nurse. How thorough she was at bath-time, and up at any moment of the night if one of her charges made the slightest cry. Of course her kennel was in the nursery. She had a genius for knowing when a cough is a thing to have no patience with and when it needs a stocking around your throat. She believed to her last day in old-fashioned remedies like rhubarb leaf, and made sounds of contempt over all this new-fangled talk about germs, and so on. It was a lesson in propriety to see her escorting the children to school, walking sedately by their side when they were well behaved, and butting them back into line if they strayed. On John's footer days she never once forgot his sweater, and she usually carried an umbrella in her mouth in case of rain.

3. There is a room in the basement of Miss Fulsom's school where the nurses wait. They sat on forms, while Nana lay on the floor, but that was the only difference. They affected to ignore her as of an inferior social status to themselves, and she despised their light talk. She resented visits to the nursery from Mrs. Darling's friends, but if they did come she first whipped off Michael's pinafore and put him into the one with blue braiding, and smoothed out Wendy and made a dash at John's hair.

4. No nursery could possibly have been conducted more correctly, and Mr. Darling knew it, yet he sometimes wondered uneasily whether the neighbours talked.

5. He had his position in the city to consider.

6. Nana also troubled him in another way. He had sometimes a feeling that she did not admire him. "I know she admires you tremendously, George," Mrs. Darling would assure him, and then she would sign to the children to be specially nice to father. Lovely dances followed, in which the only other servant, Liza, was sometimes allowed to join. Such a midget she looked in her long skirt and maid's cap, though she had sworn, when engaged, that she would never see ten again. The gaiety of those romps! And gayest of all was Mrs. Darling, who would pirouette so wildly that all you could see of her was the kiss, and then if you had dashed at her you might have got it. There never was a simpler happier family until the coming of Peter Pan.

1. "No nursery could possibly have been conducted more correctly, and Mr. Darling knew it, yet he sometimes wondered uneasily whether the neighbours talked."

   The author most likely included this information to show that Mr. Darling was worried about his

   A. reputation
   B. family
   C. children
   D. finances

2. "As they were poor, owing to the amount of milk the children drank, this nurse was a prim Newfoundland dog, called Nana, who had belonged to no one in particular until the Darlings **engaged** her."

   What does the word **engaged** mean?

   A. held the attention of, absorbed the focus
   B. entered into a conflict with, battled against someone
   C. provided with a job, employed with a job
   D. set a prior agreement, pledged to be somewhere

3. Which word best describes the tone of this story?

   A. sentimental
   B. humorous
   C. sarcastic
   D. mysterious

4. Imagine that you were going to write a reference letter for Nana. Identify and explain two reasons from the story to prove that Nana is a good nurse.

# from "NEGRO SCHOOLMASTER IN THE NEW SOUTH"
### by W.E.B. DuBois

1   ONCE upon a time I taught school in the hills of Tennessee, where the broad dark vale of the Mississippi begins to roll and crumple to greet the Alleghenies. I was a Fisk student then, and all Fisk men think that Tennessee—beyond the Veil[1]—is theirs alone, and in vacation time they sally forth in lusty bands to meet the county school commissioners. Young and happy, I too went, and I shall not soon forget that summer, ten years ago.

2   First, there was a teachers' institute at the county-seat; and there distinguished guests of the superintendent taught the teachers fractions and spelling and other mysteries—white teachers in the morning, Negroes at night. A picnic now and then, and a supper, and the rough world was softened by laughter and song. I remember how—but I wander.

3   There came a day when all the teachers left the Institute, and began the hunt for schools. I learn from hearsay (for my mother was mortally afraid of firearms) that the hunting of ducks and bears and men is wonderfully interesting, but I am sure that the man who has never hunted a country school has something to learn of the pleasures of the chase.

4   I see now the white, hot roads lazily rise and fall and wind before me under the burning July sun; I feel the deep weariness of heart and limb, as ten, eight, six miles stretch relentlessly ahead; I feel my heart sink heavily as I hear again and again, "Got a teacher? Yes." So I walked on and on—horses were too expensive—until I had wandered beyond railways, beyond stage lines, to a land of "varmints" and rattlesnakes, where the coming of a stranger was an event, and men lived and died in the shadow of one blue hill.

5   Sprinkled over hill and dale lay cabins and farmhouses, shut out from the world by the forests and the rolling hills toward the east. There I found at last a little school. Josie told me of it; she was a thin, homely girl of twenty, with a dark brown face and thick, hard hair. I had crossed the stream at Watertown, and rested under the great willows; then I had gone to the little cabin in the lot where Josie was resting on her way to town. The gaunt farmer made me welcome, and Josie, hearing my errand, told me anxiously that they wanted a school over the hill; that but once since the war had a teacher been there; that she herself longed to learn—and thus she ran on, talking fast and loud, with much earnestness and energy . . .

6   I secured the school. I remember the day I rode horseback out to the commissioner's house, with a pleasant young white fellow, who wanted the white school. The road ran down the bed of a stream; the sun laughed and the water jingled, and we rode on. "Come in," said the commissioner—"come in. Have a seat. Yes, that certificate will do. Stay to dinner. What do you want a month?" Oh, thought I, this is lucky; but even then fell the awful shadow of the Veil, for they ate first, then I—alone.

[1] For DuBois, the "Veil" refers to three things.  First, the Veil suggests the fact that black people have darker skin than white people do.  Second, the Veil refers to the fact that white people could not see blacks as "true" Americans and as persons of equal value.  Third, the Veil refers to the inability of many black people to see themselves in any other way from the way that white people saw them.

1. What is the Veil the author refers to?

    A. the land in Tennessee
    B. the lack of teachers in schools
    C. the Mississippi River
    D. the division between races

2. "I **secured** the school. I remember the day I rode horseback out to the commissioner's house, with a pleasant young white fellow, who wanted the white school."

    What does the word **secured** mean?

    A. was hired at
    B. locked up
    C. protected
    D. walked past

3. Which event in the story best shows that learning is important to Josie?

    A. Josie meets the author while going to school in town.
    B. Josie tells the author that her town needs a teacher.
    C. In the story, Josie spends a lot of time reading.
    D. The author finds Josie resting outside the school.

# SOY PROTEIN

1. Soy protein products can be good substitutes for animal products. Unlike some other beans, soy offers a "complete" protein profile. Soybeans contain all the amino acids essential to human nutrition. They must be supplied in the diet because they cannot be synthesized by the human body. Soy protein products can replace animal-based foods without requiring major adjustments elsewhere in the diet. Animal-based foods also have complete proteins, but tend to contain more fat, especially saturated fat.

2. Foreign cultures, especially Asian ones, have used soy extensively for centuries. Mainstream America has been slow to move dietary soy beyond a niche market status. In the United States, soybeans are a huge cash crop, but the product is used largely as livestock feed.

3. With the increased emphasis on healthy diets, this may be changing. Sales of soy products are up and are projected to increase due in part, say industry officials, to the Food & Drug Administration (FDA)–approved health claim. U.S. retail sales of soy foods were $4 billion in 2004.

4. Soy may seem like a new and different kind of food for many Americans. However, it actually is found in a number of products already widely consumed. For example, soybean oil accounts for 79 percent of the edible fats used annually in the United States. A glance at the ingredients for commercial mayonnaise, margarine, salad dressings, or vegetable shortening often reveals soybean oil high on the list.

5. These are some of the most common sources of soy protein:

- Tofu is made from cooked puréed soybeans processed into a custard-like cake. It has a neutral flavor and can be stir-fried, mixed into "smoothies," or blended into a cream cheese texture for use in dips or as a cheese substitute. It comes in firm, soft, and silken textures.
- "Soymilk," the name some marketers use for a soy beverage, is produced by grinding dehulled soybeans and mixing them with water to form a milk-like liquid. It can be consumed as a beverage or used in recipes as a substitute for cow's milk. Soymilk, sometimes fortified with calcium, comes plain or in flavors such as vanilla, chocolate, and coffee. For lactose-intolerant individuals, it can be a good replacement for dairy products.
- Soy flour is created by grinding roasted soybeans into a fine powder. The flour adds protein to baked goods and, because it adds moisture, it can be used as an egg substitute in these products. It also can be found in cereals, pancake mixes, frozen desserts, and other common foods.
- Textured soy protein is made from defatted soy flour, which is compressed and dehydrated. It can be used as a meat substitute or as filler in dishes like meatloaf.

- Tempeh is made from whole, cooked soybeans formed into a chewy cake and used as a meat substitute.
- Miso is a fermented soybean paste used for seasoning and in soup stock. Soy protein also is found in many "meat analog" products, such as soy sausages, burgers, franks, and cold cuts as well as in soy yogurts and cheese, all of which are intended as substitutes for their animal-based counterparts.

6    Consumers should check the labels of products to identify those most appropriate for a heart-healthy diet. Make sure the products contain enough soy protein to make a meaningful contribution to the total daily diet without being high in saturated fat and other unhealthy substances.

1. Which statement best shows that soy protein products are healthy foods?

    A. "Foreign cultures . . . have used soy extensively for centuries."
    B. "U.S. retail sales of soy foods were $4.0 billion in 2004."
    C. "Unlike some other beans, soy offers a 'complete' protein profile."
    D. "However, it actually is found in a number of products . . . widely consumed."

2. "They must be supplied in the diet because they cannot be **synthesized** by the human body."

    What does the word **synthesized** mean?

    A. absorbed
    B. produced
    C. used
    D. rejected

3. How is soymilk made?

    A. by mixing tofu with milk and then cooking the result
    B. by feeding soy to cows and then letting the milk harden
    C. by grinding soybeans and mixing them with water
    D. by using soy to replace lactose in milk in a laboratory

4. Identify and explain one way that soy products can contribute to your health. Use details from the passage to support your answer.

5. Identify and explain one reason why soybeans are a "huge cash crop" in the United States even though they are not popular in American diets. Use details from the passage to support your answer.

# THE CAPTIVE
## *from "Stories of Missouri" by John R. Musick*

1. There is no more beautiful and thrilling tale of early pioneer days than the story of Helen Patterson. She was born in Kentucky; but while she was still a child her parents removed to St. Louis County, Missouri, and lived for a time in a settlement called Cold Water, which is in St. Ferdinand township. About the year 1808 or 1809, her father took his family to the St. Charles district, and settled only a few miles from the home of the veteran backwoodsman, Daniel Boone.

2. At the time of this last removal, Helen was about eighteen years of age. She was a very religious girl, and had been taught to believe that whatever she prayed for would be granted.

3. Shortly after the family had settled in their new home, bands of prowling savages began to roam about the neighborhood. The [American] Indians would plunder the cabins of the settlers during their absence, and drive away their cattle, horses, and hogs.

4. One day business called all the Patterson family to the village, except Helen. She was busily engaged in spinning, when the house was surrounded by nine [American] Indians. Resistance was useless. She did not attempt to escape or even cry out for help; for one of the savages who spoke English gave her to understand that she would be killed if she did so.

5. She was told that she must follow the [American] Indians. They took such things as they could conveniently carry, and with their captive set off on foot through the forest, in a northwestern direction. The shrewd girl had brought a ball of yarn with her, and from this she occasionally broke off a bit and dropped it at the side of the path, as a guide to her father and friends, who she knew would soon be in pursuit.

6. This came very near being fatal to Helen, for one of the [American] Indians observed what she was doing, and raised his hatchet to [harm] her. The others interceded, but the ball of yarn was taken from her, and she was closely watched lest she might resort to some other device for marking a trail.

7. It was early in the morning when Helen was captured. Her parents were expected to return to the cabin by noon, and she reasoned that they would be in pursuit before the [American] Indians had gone very far. As the savages were on foot, and her father would no doubt follow them on horseback, he might overtake them before dark. The uneasiness expressed by her captors during the afternoon encouraged her in the belief that her friends were in pursuit.

8. A little before sunset, two of the [American] Indians went back to reconnoiter, and the other seven, with the captive, continued on in the forest. Shortly after sunset, the two [American] Indians who had fallen behind joined the others, and all held a short consultation, which the white girl could not understand.

9   The conference lasted but a few moments, and then the savages hastened forward with Helen to a creek, where the banks were sloping, and the water shallow enough for them to wade the stream. By the time they had crossed, it was quite dark. The night was cloudy, and distant thunder could occasionally be heard.

10  The [American] Indians hurried their captive to a place half a mile from the ford, and there tied her with strips of deerskin to one of the low branches of an elm. Her hands were extended above her head, and her wrists were crossed and tied so tightly that she found it impossible to release them. When they had secured her to their own satisfaction, the [American] Indians left her, assuring her that they were going back to the ford to shoot her father and his companions as they crossed it.

11  Helen was almost frantic with fear and grief. Added to the uncertainty of her own fate was the knowledge that her father and friends were marching right into an [American] Indian ambuscade.

12  In the midst of her trouble, she did not forget her pious teaching. She prayed God to send down his angels and release her. But no angel came. In her distress, the rumbling thunders in the distance were unheard, and she hardly noticed the shower until she was drenched to the skin.

13  The rain thoroughly wet the strips of deerskin with which she was tied, and as they stretched she almost unconsciously slipped her hands from them. Her prayer had been answered by the rain. She hastily untied her feet, and sped away toward the creek. Guided by the lightning's friendly glare, she crossed the stream half a mile above the ford, and hastened to meet her father and friends.

14  At every flash of lightning she strained her eyes, hoping to catch sight of them. At last moving forms were seen in the distance, but they were too far away for her to determine whether they were white men or [American] Indians. Crouching down at the root of a tree by the path, she waited until they were within a few rods of her, and then cried in a low voice, "Father! Father!"

15  "That is Helen," said Mr. Patterson.

16  She bounded to her feet, and in a moment was at his side, telling him how she had escaped. The rescuing party was composed of her father and two brothers, a neighbor named Shultz, and Nathan and Daniel M. Boone, sons of the great pioneer, Daniel Boone.

17  She told them where the [American] Indians were lying in ambush, and the frontiersmen decided to surprise them. They crossed the creek on a log, and stole down to the ford, but the [American] Indians were gone. No doubt the savages had discovered the escape of the prisoner, and, knowing that their plan to surprise the white men had failed, became frightened and fled.

18  Helen Patterson always believed it was her prayers that saved her father, her brothers, and herself in that trying hour.

1. The author most likely wrote this passage in order to

    A. convince readers that Helen was a great pioneer.
    B. tell readers a story about a girl's frightening experience.
    C. describe what it was like to be a girl on the frontier.
    D. entertain the reader with the story about a funny girl.


2. What happened to make it possible for Helen to escape?

    A. Her captors tied the deerskin too loosely around her wrists and she wiggled free.
    B. She left a path of yarn behind her so that her father and the rescuers could find her.
    C. The storm frightened her captors and she was able to run away when they hid.
    D. Rain loosened the deerskin strips around her wrists, so she was able to free herself.


3. How far do you think that Helen traveled after she was freed to find her family and friends? Do you think that a trip like this would have been difficult?

# HARRY AND HIS DOG

*by Mary Russell Mitford*

1. "Beg, Frisk, beg," said little Harry, as he sat on an inverted basket, at his grandmother's door, eating, with great satisfaction, a porringer of bread and milk. His little sister Annie sat on the ground opposite to him, now twisting her flowers into garlands, and now throwing them away.

2. "Beg, Frisk, beg!" repeated Harry, holding a bit of bread just out of the dog's reach. The obedient Frisk squatted himself on his hind legs, and held up his forepaws, waiting for master Harry to give him the tempting morsel.

3. The little boy and the little dog were great friends. Frisk loved him dearly, much better than he did any one else, perhaps, because he remembered that Harry was his earliest and firmest friend during a time of great trouble.

4. Poor Frisk had come as a stray dog to Milton, the place where Harry lived. If he could have told his own story, it would probably have been a very pitiful one, of kicks and cuffs, of hunger and foul weather.

5. Certain it is, he made his appearance at the very door where Harry was now sitting, in miserable plight, wet, dirty, and half starved; and there he met Harry, who took a fancy to him, and Harry's grandmother, who drove him off with a broom.

6. Harry, at length, obtained permission for the little dog to remain as a sort of outdoor pensioner, and fed him with stray bones and cold potatoes, and such things as he could get for him. He also provided him with a little basket to sleep in, the very same which, turned up, afterward served Harry for a seat.

7. After a while, having proved his good qualities by barking away a set of pilferers, who were making an attack on the great pear tree, he was admitted into the house, and became one of its most vigilant and valued inmates. He could fetch or carry either by land or water; would pick up a thimble or a ball of cotton, if little Annie should happen to drop them; or take Harry's dinner to school for him with perfect honesty.

8. "Beg, Frisk, beg!" said Harry, and gave him, after long waiting, the expected morsel. Frisk was satisfied, but Harry was not. The little boy, though a good-humored fellow in the main, had turns of naughtiness, which were apt to last him all day, and this promised to prove one of his worst. It was a holiday, and in the afternoon his cousins, Jane and William, were to come and see him and Annie; and the pears were to be gathered, and the children were to have a treat.

9. Harry, in his impatience, thought the morning would never be over. He played such pranks—buffeting Frisk, cutting the curls off of Annie's doll, and finally breaking his grandmother's spectacles—that before his visitors arrived, indeed, almost immediately after dinner, he contrived to be sent to bed in disgrace.

10   Poor Harry! There he lay, rolling and kicking, while Jane, and William, and Annie were busy gathering the fine, mellow pears. William was up in the tree, gathering and shaking. Annie and Jane were catching them in their aprons, or picking them up from the ground, now piling them in baskets, and now eating the nicest and ripest, while Frisk was barking gaily among them, as if he were catching pears, too!

11   Poor Harry! He could hear all this glee and merriment through the open window, as he lay in bed. The storm of passion having subsided, there he lay weeping and disconsolate, a grievous sob bursting forth every now and then, as he heard the loud peals of childish laughter, and as he thought how he should have laughed, and how happy he should have been, had he not forfeited all his pleasure by his own bad conduct.

12   He wondered if Annie would not be so good-natured as to bring him a pear. All on a sudden, he heard a little foot on the stair, "pitapat," and he thought she was coming. "Pitapat" came the foot, nearer and nearer, and at last a small head peeped, half afraid, through the half-open door.

13   But it was not Annie's head; it was Frisk's—poor Frisk, whom Harry had been teasing all the morning, and who came into the room wagging his tail, with a great pear in his mouth; and, jumping upon the bed, he laid it in the little boy's hand.


1. Which word best describes the relationship between Harry and Frisk?

   A. distant
   B. competitive
   C. jealous
   D. loyal


2. What is this passage mostly about?

   A. a family picking pears from a tree
   B. a little boy who was sent to bed
   C. a dog that is faithful to his owner
   D. a girl that teases her little brother

3. "After a while, having proved his good qualities by barking away a set of pilferers, who were making an attack on the great pear tree, he was admitted into the house, and became one of its most vigilant and valued **inmates**."

   What does the word **inmates** mean?

   A. prisoners
   B. inhabitants
   C. friends
   D. children

4. Which sentence from the passage most strongly develops a mood of pity?

   A. " 'Beg, Frisk, beg!' said Harry, and gave him, after long waiting, the expected morsel."
   B. "All on a sudden, he heard a little foot on the stair, 'pitapat,' and he thought she was coming."
   C. "Harry, in his impatience, thought the morning would never be over."
   D. "Poor Harry! He could hear all this glee and merriment through the open window, as he lay in bed."

5. Frisk is allowed to stay with Henry's family because he

   A. brought Henry his dinner at school every day
   B. helped Henry's grandmother to find her lost spectacles
   C. fetched Annie the tools she needed while she was sewing
   D. frightened away people who were stealing pears

6. What will Harry most likely do next in the passage?

   A. punish Frisk for stealing
   B. share the pear with Frisk
   C. go outside and pick more pears
   D. return the pear to his cousins

7. Do you think that someone had told Frisk to bring Harry the pear or that Frisk had brought it on his own? Use details from the passage to support your answer.

# from "THE GOLDEN TOUCH"
## by Nathaniel Hawthorne

1. Once upon a time, there lived a very rich man, and a king besides, whose name was Midas. He had a little daughter, whom nobody but myself ever heard of, and whose name I either never knew, or have entirely forgotten. So, because I love odd names for little girls, I choose to call her Marygold.

2. This King Midas was fonder of gold than of anything else in the world. He valued his royal crown chiefly because it was composed of that precious metal. If he loved anything better, or half so well, it was the one little maiden who played so merrily around her father's footstool. But the more Midas loved his daughter, the more did he desire and seek for wealth. He thought, foolish man! that the best thing he could possibly do for this dear child would be to bequeath her the largest pile of glistening coin that had ever been heaped together since the world was made.

3. Thus he gave all his thoughts and all his time to this one purpose. If ever he happened to gaze for an instant at the gold-tinted clouds of sunset, he wished that they were real gold, and that they could be squeezed safely into his strong box. When little Marygold ran to meet him, with a bunch of buttercups and dandelions, he used to say, "Pooh, pooh, child! If these flowers were as golden as they look, they would be worth the plucking!"

4. At length (as people always grow more and more foolish, unless they take care to grow wiser and wiser) Midas had got to be so exceedingly unreasonable, that he could scarcely bear to see or touch any object that was not gold. He made it his custom, therefore, to pass a large portion of every day in a dark and dreary apartment, under ground, at the basement of his palace. It was here that he kept his wealth. To this dismal hole—for it was little better than a dungeon—Midas betook himself, whenever he wanted to be particularly happy.

5. Here, after carefully locking the door, he would take a bag of gold coin, or a gold cup as big as a washbowl, or a heavy golden bar, or a peck measure of gold dust, and bring them from the obscure corners of the room into the one bright and narrow sunbeam that fell from the dungeon-like window. He valued the sunbeam for no other reason but that his treasure would not shine without its help.

6. And then would he reckon over the coins in the bag; toss up the bar, and catch it as it came down; sift the gold dust through his fingers; look at the funny image of his own face, as reflected in the burnished circumference of the cup; and whisper to himself, "O Midas, rich King Midas, what a happy man art thou!"

7. Midas was enjoying himself in his treasure room, one day, as usual, when he perceived a shadow fall over the heaps of gold. Looking up, he beheld the figure of a stranger, standing in the bright and narrow sunbeam! It was a young man, with a cheerful and ruddy face.

8   Whether it was that the imagination of King Midas threw a yellow tinge over everything, or whatever the cause might be, he could not help fancying that the smile with which the stranger regarded him had a kind of golden brightness in it.

9   Certainly, there was now a brighter gleam upon all the piled-up treasures than before. Even the remotest corners had their share of it, and were lighted up, when the stranger smiled, as with tips of flame and sparkles of fire.

10  As Midas knew that he had carefully turned the key in the lock, and that no mortal strength could possibly break into his treasure room; he, of course, concluded that his visitor must be something more than mortal.

11  Midas had met such beings before now, and was not sorry to meet one of them again. The stranger's aspect, indeed, was so good-humored and kindly, if not beneficent, that it would have been unreasonable to suspect him of intending any mischief. It was far more probable that he came to do Midas a favor. And what could that favor be, unless to multiply his heaps of treasure?

12  The stranger gazed about the room; and, when his lustrous smile had glistened upon all the golden objects that were there, he turned again to Midas.

13  "You are a wealthy man, friend Midas!" he observed. "I doubt whether any other four walls on earth contain so much gold as you have contrived to pile up in this room."

14  "I have done pretty well—pretty well," answered Midas, in a discontented tone. "But, after all, it is but a trifle, when you consider that it has taken me my whole lifetime to get it together. If one could live a thousand years, he might have time to grow rich!"

15  "What!" exclaimed the stranger. "Then you are not satisfied?"

16  Midas shook his head.

17  "And pray, what would satisfy you?" asked the stranger. "Merely for the curiosity of the thing, I should be glad to know."

18  Why did the stranger ask this question? Did he have it in his power to gratify the king's wishes? It was an odd question, to say the least.

19  Midas paused and meditated. He felt sure that this stranger, with such a golden luster in his good-humored smile, had come hither with both the power and the purpose of gratifying his utmost wishes. Now, therefore, was the fortunate moment, when he had but to speak, and obtain whatever possible or seemingly impossible thing, it might come into his head to ask. So he thought, and thought, and thought, and heaped up one golden mountain upon another, in his imagination, without being able to imagine them big enough.

20  At last a bright idea occurred to King Midas.

21  Raising his head, he looked the lustrous stranger in the face.

22  "Well, Midas," observed his visitor, "I see that you have at length hit upon something that will satisfy you. Tell me your wish."

23  "It is only this," replied Midas. "I am weary of collecting my treasures with so much trouble, and beholding the heap so diminutive, after I have done my best. I wish everything that I touch to be changed to gold!"


1. Which theme best applies to the passage?

    A. It's easier to spend than to earn.
    B. Don't put your trust in strangers.
    C. Be happy with what you have.
    D. Appearances can be deceiving.


2. Which word best describes King Midas when he makes his wish?

    A. curious
    B. stubborn
    C. indifferent
    D. selfish


3. "Here, after carefully locking the door, he would take a bag of gold coin, or a gold cup as big as a washbowl, or a heavy golden bar, or a peck measure of gold dust, and bring them from the **obscure** corners of the room into the one bright and narrow sunbeam that fell from the dungeon-like window."

    What does the word **obscure** mean?

    A. dim
    B. worthless
    C. humble
    D. obvious

4. Why did the author most likely choose the name "Marygold" for King Midas's daughter? Use details from the passage to support your answer.

5. What do you think of King Midas and his wish? Would you ever make a wish like that? Use details from the passage to support your answer.

# from "THE VELVETEEN RABBIT"
## *by Margery Williams Bianco*

1. The Rabbit sighed. He thought it would be a long time before this magic called Real happened to him. He longed to become Real, to know what it felt like; and yet the idea of growing shabby and losing his eyes and whiskers was rather sad. He wished that he could become it without these uncomfortable things happening to him.

2. There was a person called Nana who ruled the nursery. Sometimes she took no notice of the playthings lying about, and sometimes, for no reason whatever, she went swooping about like a great wind and hustled them away in cupboards. She called this "tidying up," and the playthings all hated it, especially the tin ones.

3. The Rabbit didn't mind it so much, for wherever he was thrown he came down soft.

4. One evening, when the Boy was going to bed, he couldn't find the china dog that always slept with him. Nana was in a hurry, and it was too much trouble to hunt for china dogs at bedtime, so she simply looked about her, and seeing that the toy cupboard stood open, she made a swoop.

5. "Here," she said, "take your old Bunny! He'll do to sleep with you!" And she dragged the Rabbit out by one ear, and put him into the Boy's arms.

6. That night, and for many nights after, the Velveteen Rabbit slept in the Boy's bed. At first he found it uncomfortable, for the Boy hugged him very tight, and sometimes he rolled over on him, and sometimes he pushed him so far under the pillow that the Rabbit could scarcely breathe. And he missed, too, those long moonlight hours in the nursery, when all the house was silent, and his talks with the Skin Horse.

7. But very soon he grew to like it, for the Boy used to talk to him, and made nice tunnels for him under the bedclothes that he said were like the burrow the real rabbits lived in. And they had splendid games together, in whispers, when Nana had gone away to her supper and left the night-light burning on the mantelpiece. And when the Boy dropped off to sleep, the Rabbit would snuggle down close under his little warm chin and dream, with the Boy's hands clasped close round him, all night long.

8. And so time went on, and the little Rabbit was very happy—so happy that he never noticed how his beautiful velveteen fur was getting shabbier and shabbier, and his tail becoming unsewn, and all the pink rubbed off his nose where the Boy had kissed him.

1. "And when the Boy dropped off to sleep, the Rabbit would snuggle down close under his little warm chin and dream, with the Boy's hands clasped close round him, all night long."

    The Rabbit and the Boy are alike in that they both

    A. have big dreams for the future.
    B. enjoy talks with the Skin Horse.
    C. find comfort in each other.
    D. dislike when Nana tidies up.

2. Which statement best shows what is happening to Rabbit at the end of the passage?

    A. He is becoming Real.
    B. He is being forgotten.
    C. He is missed by the other toys.
    D. He is lonely without his friends.

3. Why doesn't Rabbit notice that he is becoming shabby?

    A. He can't compare himself to other toys.
    B. It is too dark to see under the covers.
    C. There are no mirrors in the bedroom.
    D. He is too happy to care what he looks like.

4. Why does the Rabbit come to like sleeping in the Boy's bed? Use information from the passage to support your answer.

5. Would you want to become Real if you were the Rabbit? Use information from the passage to support your answer.

# CESAR CHAVEZ

1. Cesar Chavez was born in North Gila Valley, near Yuma, Arizona. He was one of six children. His parents owned a ranch and a small grocery store. During the Great Depression in the 1930s, they lost everything. In order to survive, Cesar Chavez and his family became migrant farm workers. They traveled around California to find work. It was very hard. They could not live in the same place for long. They had to follow the crops. The Chavez family would pick peas and lettuce in the winter, cherries and beans in the spring, corn and grapes in the summer, and cotton in the fall.

2. Working conditions for migrant workers were harsh and often unsafe. Their wages were low, and it was difficult to support a family. Cesar's family frequently did not have access to such basic needs as clean water or toilets. A large number of migrant workers were Mexican American. They also often faced prejudice. Their children had to skip school to earn wages to help support the family.

3. As his family moved from place to place to find work, Cesar Chavez attended about thirty schools in California. After the eighth grade, Cesar had to quit school to support his ailing parents.

4. Cesar's life growing up had a big impact on what he did with the rest of his life. In 1948, he married a woman who also was from a family of migrant farm workers. By 1959, the couple had eight children. Chavez, who had little education and training, was forced to return to farm work.

5. Cesar Chavez spent most of his life working on farms in California. Pay was low and comforts were few. He wanted to improve the situation. In the 1950s, he started organizing agricultural workers into a labor union that would demand higher pay and better working conditions from their employers. In 1962, Chavez and fellow organizer Dolores Huerta founded the Farm Workers Association.

6. In 1965, Chavez and Huerta agreed to honor a walkout by farm workers in Delano, California. Workers were asked not to work for the Delano grape growers. In Spanish, this strike was called a *huelga* (pronounced WELL-guh).

7. The strike that started in 1965 lasted for five years. It inspired a nationwide boycott of California grapes that was supported throughout the country.

8. There was another grape boycott in the mid-1970s. It forced growers to support the 1975 Agricultural Labor Relations Act. The United Farm Workers fought grape producers for better working conditions. Chavez and Huerta led them. They used nonviolent tactics such as protest marches, strikes, and boycotts. These tactics were usually successful. The farm workers and the growers signed agreements.

1. Cesar Chavez's main problem was that

    A. his family moved around the country a lot.
    B. he felt that farm workers were treated unfairly.
    C. he had to leave school because he needed work.
    D. his father lost his farm during the Depression.


2. What does this passage suggest about Cesar Chavez?

    A. He lived his life without hope.
    B. He was an irresponsible person.
    C. He inspired many people.
    D. He led an uninteresting life.


3. How is the information in this passage organized?

    A. The events of Cesar Chavez's life are presented in the order in which they occurred.
    B. Questions about the California grape boycott are answered by Cesar Chavez.
    C. An opinion about the Farm Workers Association is supported with researched facts.
    D. A description of Farm Workers Association is followed by the reasons for its formation.


4. The author most likely wrote this passage in order to

    A. entertain by telling a story about farmers working in California
    B. tell how Cesar Chavez formed the United Farm Workers
    C. convince people not to buy grapes from Delano, California
    D. explain what life was like for people in the Great Depression

5. Why was Cesar Chavez's work important? Use information from the passage to support your answer.

# EARTH'S WATER

1. How much water is there on (and in) the earth?

2. As you know, the earth is a watery place. About 70 percent of the earth's surface is water-covered. Water also exists in the air as water vapor and in the ground as soil moisture and in aquifers. Thanks to the water cycle, our planet's water supply is constantly moving from one place to another and from one form to another. Things would get pretty stale without the water cycle!

3. When you take a look at the water around you, you see water in streams, rivers, and lakes. You see water sitting on the surface of the earth. Naturally, this water is known as "surface water." Your view of the water cycle might be that when rain falls, it fills up the rivers and lakes. However, how would you account for the flow in rivers after weeks without rain? The answer is that there is more to our water supply than just surface water. There is also plenty of water beneath our feet. It is stored in aquifers.

4. Even though you may only notice water on the earth's surface, there is much more water stored in the ground than there is on the surface. In fact, some of the water you see flowing in rivers comes from seepage of ground water into riverbeds. Water from precipitation continually seeps into the ground to recharge the aquifers. At the same time, water from underground aquifers continually recharges rivers through seepage.

5. People make use of both kinds of water. In the United States in 1995, we used about 321 billion gallons per day of surface water and about 77 billion gallons per day of ground water. In a way, that underestimates the importance of ground water. Not only does ground water help to keep our rivers and lakes full, it also provides water for people in places where visible water is scarce, such as in the desert towns of the western United States. Without ground water, people would be sand surfing in Palm Springs, California, instead of playing golf!

6. Just how much water is there on (and in) the earth? Here are some numbers you can think about. The total water supply of the world is 326 million cubic miles. If all of the world's water were poured on the United States, it would cover the land to a depth of 90 miles.

7. Of the fresh water on earth, much more is stored in the ground than is available in lakes and rivers. More than two million cubic miles of fresh water is stored in the earth, most within one half-mile of the surface. Contrast that with the 60,000 cubic miles of water stored as fresh water in lakes, inland seas, and rivers. If you really want to find fresh water, however, most is stored in the seven million cubic miles of water found in glaciers and ice caps, mainly in the polar regions and in Greenland.

1. What is this passage mostly about?

    A. the water supply of aquifers
    B. the water found in riverbeds
    C. the water found in glaciers
    D. the water supply of the earth

2. The "Earth's Water" passage is most similar to

    A. a set of detailed instructions
    B. an editorial in a newspaper
    C. an article in a textbook
    D. an advertisement in a magazine

3. The author most likely included the information in the fourth paragraph of the passage to

    A. discuss the fresh water found in glaciers
    B. show readers how much water is used daily
    C. explain how aquifers recharge the water supply
    D. encourage readers to use fresh water sparingly

4. Explain why we still might experience water shortages even though the water cycle constantly recharges the water supply. Use information from the passage to support your answer.

# TRAVELING ABROAD

1. Millions of United States citizens travel abroad each year and use their U.S. passports. When you travel abroad, the odds are in your favor that you will have a safe and incident-free trip. However, crime and violence, as well as unexpected difficulties, do befall U.S. citizens in all parts of the world. No one is better able to tell you this than U.S. consular officers. They work in the more than 250 U.S. embassies and consulates around the globe. Every day of the year, U.S. embassies and consulates receive calls from American citizens in distress.

2. Fortunately, most problems can be solved over the telephone or when a U.S. citizen visits the Consular Section of the nearest U.S. embassy or consulate. There are, however, less fortunate occasions when U.S. consular officers are called on to meet U.S. citizens at foreign police stations, hospitals, prisons, and even at morgues. In these cases, the assistance that consular officers can offer is specific but limited.

3. In the hope of helping you to avoid unhappy meetings with consular officers when you go abroad, we have prepared the following travel tips. Please have a safe trip.

- ❏ Safety begins when you pack. To avoid being a target, dress conservatively. A flashy wardrobe or one that is too casual can mark you as a tourist. As much as possible, avoid the appearance of wealth.

- ❏ Always try to travel light. If you do, you can move more quickly. You will be more likely to have a free hand. You will also be less tired and less likely to set your luggage down, leaving it unattended.

- ❏ Carry the minimum amount of valuables necessary for your trip and plan a place or places to conceal them. Your passport, cash, and credit cards are most secure when locked in a hotel safe. When you have to carry them on your person, you may wish to conceal them in several places. Avoid putting them all in one wallet or pouch. Bring travelers checks and one or two major credit cards instead of cash.

- ❏ Avoid handbags, fanny packs, and outside pockets, which are easy targets for thieves. Inside pockets and a sturdy shoulder bag with the strap worn across your chest are somewhat safer. One of the safest places to carry valuables is in a pouch or money belt worn under your clothing.

- ❏ If you wear glasses, pack an extra pair. Bring them along with any medicines you need in your carry-on luggage. To avoid problems when passing through customs, keep medicines in their original, labeled containers. Bring a copy of your prescriptions and the generic names for the drugs. If a medication is unusual or contains narcotics, carry a letter from your doctor attesting to your need to take the drug. If you have any doubt about the legality of carrying a certain drug into a country, consult the embassy or consulate of that country first.

❑ Pack an extra set of passport photos along with a photocopy of your passport information page to make replacement of your passport easier in the event that it is lost or stolen.

❑ Put your name, address, and telephone number inside and outside of each piece of luggage. Use covered luggage tags to avoid casual observation of your identity or nationality and, if possible, lock your luggage.

❑ Consider getting a telephone calling card. It is a convenient way of keeping in touch. If you have one, verify that you can use it from your overseas location(s). Access numbers to U.S. operators are published in many international newspapers. Find out your access number before you go.

1. "Safety begins when you pack. To avoid being a target, dress **conservatively**. A flashy wardrobe or one that is too casual can mark you as a tourist."

   The information in these sentences suggests that to dress **conservatively** is to dress

   A. elegantly.
   B. sharply.
   C. colorfully.
   D. properly.

2. Which statement best describes the author's viewpoint about traveling abroad?

   A. There are steps that travelers can take to stay safe.
   B. Travelers should wear their most comfortable clothes.
   C. There is very little help for travelers who go overseas.
   D. Travelers should never bring any medications overseas.

3. What is the purpose of the bullets throughout the passage?
   A. to indicate when a tip has been recommended by a U.S. embassy
   B. to show when a tip applies to travel within the United States
   C. to identify only the most important tips
   D. to separate each tip into its own section

4. Pretend that you have been chosen to give a talk to your class about traveling abroad. Write down two important safety tips your classmates should know about. Use information from the selection to support your response.

# CENSORSHIP IN MUSIC

1. Censorship in music is a topic that has brought about much controversy in the past few decades. Some people believe that music should be censored so that it will not be offensive to anyone. Others feel that music should never be subject to censorship since it is an expression of artistic creativity. Still others fall somewhere in between, opining that at least the most obscene and offensive material should be restricted in some way.

2. Whether or not a person finds a piece of music obscene depends largely on his or her moral or religious beliefs. These views change from generation to generation. Those people who believe that music should be censored feel that some of the language music artists use is vulgar and crude. They further this opinion by pointing out that some of this music is played on the radio and on television; therefore, it is accessible to the public.

3. Many parents do not wish for their children to hear foul language. Today, foul language which might be played on public radio broadcasts and on television is edited out in some way. Some artists make two versions of their songs: one uncensored for the album, and another censored for television and radio. Even cable television, which is paid for by the viewers monthly, is subject to this form of censorship, although pay-per-view-type channels are not.

4. Preventing or punishing speech is a clear violation of the First Amendment, which says: "Congress shall make no law abridging the freedom of speech or of the press." Therefore, the First Amendment guarantees the right to freedom of speech. Censorship violates this right, which is the complaint made by many musicians. Some artists express their feelings directly through their music, projecting their emotions for the world to hear. By censoring their true words and forcing them to modify their lyrics, censors in essence limit the artist's right to express himself or herself.

5. Does censoring music really solve the problem of exposing children to explicit language? Many children hear foul language from friends, older siblings, or parents at an early age. Just by walking down the street, they can encounter any number of colorful phrases, not to mention the obscene actions of people that they can witness. Children may revere someone who uses obscene language, but that person could just as easily be a parent or sibling and is not necessarily a musician. Eventually, everyone will be exposed to language they do not find acceptable. It is not solely the music artists' responsibility to restrict themselves for the sake of children. Censorship, in this case, is strongly biased and cannot compensate for the number of other places and people that a child could come across to encounter this type of language.

6. The question is: Who should decide what you read or view—the church, the government . . . or you? The answer to that question is *you*. Censorship on television channels such as Nickelodeon® or PBS® is understandable due to the fact that they

mainly broadcast young children's programming. However, it is unnecessary to censor stations generally viewed (or listened to) by older audiences.

7   A few years ago, angry mothers and fathers sued artists and/or record companies for releasing albums that, without making note of the fact, contained explicit lyrics. They were concerned that their children might repeat these newly-learned words to teachers, principals, friends, and/or siblings. (Those same parents, I'm sure, used those same foul words in front of their children at one time or another.) By law, record companies are now required to put stickers on cassette tapes and compact discs that say: "PARENTAL ADVISORY. EXPLICIT LYRICS."

8   Many parents also complained that the art on many album covers and within the contents of the albums themselves was too vulgar. For example, the Black Crowes' *Amorica* album, after its first release, was blasted by the media. The band chose to rerelease the album with the disputed sections of the cover blacked out completely.

9   If parents do not wish for their children to hear foul language, they should more closely supervise their children. While the government has taken an active role in this fight, it should not be expected to shoulder the full responsibility of limiting each child's access to adult themes and language. If a concerned parent is worried about her child's exposure to foul language and controversial music, it is not the artist's job to limit his creative freedom. The parent can always screen the album before allowing her child to hear it. If she doesn't like the content, she can always return it and decline her child's request to own it.

10  Many parents nowadays would rather have outside agencies limit their children than have to take on the responsibility themselves. Unfortunately, this attitude leads to the restriction—and sometimes the abolishment—of other people's freedoms. Under the First Amendment, we all have the right to express ourselves freely and openly. Censorship serves to kill that right and directly contradicts what it means to be an American.

1. Why did parents sue record companies and artists?
    A. Artists' lyrics may have caused children to use foul language.
    B. Record companies encouraged the use of foul lyrics on albums.
    C. The parents wanted album covers to be blacked out completely.
    D. Record companies labeled albums which contained foul content.

2. What is this passage mostly about?

   A. how the government interprets the First Amendment
   B. why the government should censor music more
   C. how censorship violates citizens' and artists' rights
   D. what parents should know about their children's music

3. What does this passage suggest about censorship?

   A. It is necessary on public radio stations.
   B. It is needed most in media for children.
   C. It is necessary for some artists' work.
   D. It is needed most on cable TV shows.

4. Which statement best describes the author's viewpoint about censorship?

   A. Censorship limits musicians' ability to express themselves.
   B. Censoring songs stops children from using bad language.
   C. Censorship decreases album sales in some places.
   D. Artists should make two versions of all new songs.

5. The most uncensored version of a musician's work can most likely be found by

   A. looking at the album cover.
   B. listening to the artist's album.
   C. watching a video on television.
   D. listening to the artist on the radio.

6. The "Censorship in Music" passage is most similar to

   A. an interview with a musician
   B. an editorial in a newspaper
   C. an informational brochure
   D. a story for teenage children

7. The author most likely wrote this passage in order to

   A. analyze all the ways in which censorship can be harmful
   B. instruct the readers on how their rights are being violated
   C. persuade the readers to form an opinion against censorship
   D. inform the readers of the correct way to raise their children

8. Why should parents supervise what their children listen to?

    A. so that they have something to talk about
    B. because government does not do it
    C. because most artists are controversial
    D. so that they can decide what is appropriate


9. "Preventing or punishing speech is a clear violation of the First Amendment, which says: 'Congress shall make no law **abridging** the freedom of speech or of the press.'"

    What does the word **abridging** mean?

    A. limiting
    B. crossing
    C. removing
    D. concerning

10. Explain whether censorship rules should or should not apply equally to lyrics that are racist, lyrics that are violent, and lyrics that contain foul language. Based on the argument presented in this passage, what do you think the author of this article would say? Use information from the passage to support your answer

11. The author of this article has strong opinions on the role censorship plays in limiting people's freedoms. Do you think that the argument is at all biased? Why or why not? Use information from the passage to support your answer.

# from "THE FINANCIER"
## by Theodore Dreiser

1   It was in his thirteenth year that young Cowperwood entered into his first business venture.

2   Walking along Front Street one day, a street of importing and wholesale establishments, he saw an auctioneer's flag hanging out before a wholesale grocery and from the interior came the auctioneer's voice: "What am I bid for this exceptional lot of Java coffee, twenty-two bags all told, which is now selling in the market for seven dollars and thirty-two cents a bag wholesale? What am I bid? What am I bid? The whole lot must go as one. What am I bid?"

3   "Eighteen dollars," suggested a trader standing near the door, more to start the bidding than anything else. Frank paused.

4   "Twenty-two!" called another.

5   "Thirty!" a third. "Thirty-five!" a fourth, and so up to seventy-five, less than half of what it was worth.

6   "I'm bid seventy-five! I'm bid seventy-five!" called the auctioneer, loudly. "Any other offers? Going once at seventy-five; am I offered eighty? Going twice at seventy-five, and"—he paused, one hand raised dramatically. Then he brought it down with a slap in the palm of the other—"sold to Mr. Silas Gregory for seventy-five. Make a note of that, Jerry," he called to his red-haired, freckle-faced clerk beside him. Then he turned to another lot of grocery staples—this time starch, eleven barrels of it.

7   Young Cowperwood was making a rapid calculation. If, as the auctioneer said, coffee was worth seven dollars and thirty-two cents a bag in the open market, and this buyer was getting this coffee for seventy-five dollars, he was making then and there eighty-six dollars and four cents, to say nothing of what his profit would be if he sold it at retail. As he recalled, his mother was paying twenty-eight cents a pound. He drew nearer, his books tucked under his arm, and watched these operations closely. The starch, as he soon heard, was valued at ten dollars a barrel, and it only brought six. Some kegs of vinegar were knocked down at one-third their value, and so on. He began to wish he could bid; but he had no money, just a little pocket change. The auctioneer noticed him standing almost directly under his nose, and was impressed with the stolidity—stolidity—of the boy's expression.

8   "I am going to offer you now a fine lot of Castile soap—seven cases, no less—which, as you know, if you know anything about soap, is now selling at fourteen cents a bar. This soap is worth anywhere at this moment eleven dollars and seventy-five cents a case. What am I bid? What am I bid? What am I bid?" He was talking fast in the usual style of auctioneers, with much unnecessary emphasis; but Cowperwood was not unduly impressed. He was already rapidly calculating for himself. Seven cases

at eleven dollars and seventy-five cents would be worth just eighty-two dollars and twenty-five cents; and if it went at half—if it went at half—

9   "Twelve dollars," commented one bidder.

10  "Fifteen," bid another.

11  "Twenty," called a third.

12  "Twenty-five," a fourth.

13  Then it came to dollar raises, for Castile soap was not such a vital commodity.

14  "Twenty-six."

15  "Twenty-seven."

16  "Twenty-eight."

17  "Twenty-nine." There was a pause.

18  "Thirty," observed young Cowperwood, decisively.

19  The auctioneer, a short lean faced, spare man with bushy hair and an incisive eye, looked at him curiously and almost incredulously but without pausing. He had, somehow, in spite of himself, been impressed by the boy's peculiar eye. Now he felt, without knowing why, that the offer was probably legitimate enough, and that the boy had the money. He might be the son of a grocer.

20  "I'm bid thirty! I'm bid thirty! I'm bid thirty for this fine lot of Castile soap. It's a fine lot. It's worth fourteen cents a bar. Will any one bid thirty-one? Will any one bid thirty-one? Will any one bid thirty-one?"

21  "Thirty-one," said a voice.

22  "Thirty-two," replied Cowperwood. The same process was repeated.

23  "I'm bid thirty-two! I'm bid thirty-two! I'm bid thirty-two! Will anybody bid thirty-three? It's fine soap. Seven cases of fine Castile soap. Will anybody bid thirty-three?"

24  Young Cowperwood's mind was working. He had no money with him; but his father was teller of the Third National Bank, and he could quote him as reference. He could sell all of his soap to the family grocer, surely; or, if not, to other grocers. Other people were anxious to get this soap at this price. Why not he?

25  The auctioneer paused.

26. "Thirty-two once! Am I bid thirty-three? Thirty-two twice! Am I bid thirty-three? Thirty-two three times! Seven fine cases of soap. Am I bid anything more? Once, twice! Three times! Am I bid anything more?"—his hand was up again—"and sold to Mr.—?" He leaned over and looked curiously into the face of his young bidder.

27. "Frank Cowperwood, son of the teller of the Third National Bank," replied the boy, decisively.

28. "Oh, yes," said the man, fixed by his glance.

29. "Will you wait while I run up to the bank and get the money?"

30. "Yes. Don't be gone long. If you're not here in an hour I'll sell it again."

31. Young Cowperwood made no reply. He hurried out and ran fast; first, to his mother's grocer, whose store was within a block of his home.

32. Thirty feet from the door he slowed up, put on a nonchalant air, and strolling in, looked about for Castile soap. There it was, the same kind, displayed in a box and looking just as his soap looked.

33. "How much is this a bar, Mr. Dalrymple?" he inquired.

34. "Sixteen cents," replied that worthy.

35. "If I could sell you seven boxes for sixty-two dollars just like this, would you take them?"

36. "The same soap?"

37. "Yes, sir."

38. Mr. Dalrymple calculated a moment.

39. "Yes, I think I would," he replied, cautiously.

40. "Would you pay me to-day?"

41. "I'd give you my note for it. Where is the soap?"

42. He was perplexed and somewhat astonished by this unexpected proposition on the part of his neighbor's son. He knew Mr. Cowperwood well—and Frank also.

43. "Will you take it if I bring it to you to-day?"

44. "Yes, I will," he replied. "Are you going into the soap business?"

45   "No. But I know where I can get some of that soap cheap."

46   He hurried out again and ran to his father's bank. It was after banking hours; but he knew how to get in, and he knew that his father would be glad to see him make thirty dollars. He only wanted to borrow the money for a day.

47   "What's the trouble, Frank?" asked his father, looking up from his desk when he appeared, breathless and red faced.

48   "I want you to loan me thirty-two dollars! Will you?"

49   "Why, yes, I might. What do you want to do with it?"

50   "I want to buy some soap—seven bars of Castile soap. I know where I can get it and sell it. Mr. Dalrymple will take it. He's already offered me sixty-two for it. I can get it for thirty-two. Will you let me have the money? I've got to run back and pay the auctioneer."

51   His father smiled. This was the most business-like attitude he had seen his son manifest.

52   He was so keen, so alert for a boy of thirteen.

53   "Why, Frank," he said, going over to a drawer where some bills were, "are you going to become a financier already? You're sure you're not going to lose on this? You know what you're doing, do you?"

54   "You let me have the money, father, will you?" he pleaded. "I'll show you in a little bit. Just let me have it. You can trust me."

55   He was like a young hound on the scent of game. His father could not resist his appeal.

56   "Why, certainly, Frank," he replied. "I'll trust you." And he counted out six five-dollar certificates of the Third National's own issue and two ones. "There you are."

57   Frank ran out of the building with a briefly spoken thanks and returned to the auction room as fast as his legs would carry him. When he came in, sugar was being auctioned. He made his way to the auctioneer's clerk.

58   "I want to pay for that soap," he suggested.

59   "Now?"

60   "Yes. Will you give me a receipt?"

61   "Yep."

62 "Do you deliver this?"

63 "No. No delivery. You have to take it away in twenty-four hours."

64 That difficulty did not trouble him.

65 "All right," he said, and pocketed his paper testimony of purchase.

66 The auctioneer watched him as he went out. In half an hour he was back with a drayman—an idle levee-wharf hanger-on who was waiting for a job.

67 Frank had bargained with him to deliver the soap for sixty cents. In still another half-hour he was before the door of the astonished Mr. Dalrymple whom he had come out and look at the boxes before attempting to remove them. His plan was to have them carried on to his own home if the operation for any reason failed to go through. Though it was his first great venture, he was cool as glass.

68 "Yes," said Mr. Dalrymple, scratching his gray head reflectively. "Yes, that's the same soap. I'll take it. I'll be as good as my word. Where'd you get it, Frank?"

69 "At Bixom's auction up here," he replied, frankly and blandly.

70 Mr. Dalrymple had the drayman bring in the soap; and after some formality—because the agent in this case was a boy—made out his note at thirty days and gave it to him.

71 Frank thanked him and pocketed the note. He decided to go back to his father's bank and discount it, as he had seen others doing, thereby paying his father back and getting his own profit in ready money. It couldn't be done ordinarily on any day after business hours; but his father would make an exception in his case.

72 He hurried back, whistling; and his father glanced up smiling when he came in.

73 "Well, Frank, how'd you make out?" he asked.

74 "Here's a note at thirty days," he said, producing the paper Dalrymple had given him. "Do you want to discount that for me? You can take your thirty-two out of that."

75 His father examined it closely. "Sixty-two dollars!" he observed. "Mr. Dalrymple! That's good paper! Yes, I can. It will cost you ten per cent," he added, jestingly. "Why don't you just hold it, though? I'll let you have the thirty-two dollars until the end of the month."

76 "Oh, no," said his son, "you discount it and take your money. I may want mine."

77 His father smiled at his business-like air. "All right," he said. "I'll fix it to-morrow. Tell me just how you did this." And his son told him.

78  At seven o'clock that evening Frank's mother heard about it, and in due time Uncle Seneca.

79  "What'd I tell you, Cowperwood?" he asked. "He has stuff in him, that youngster. Look out for him."

80  Mrs. Cowperwood looked at her boy curiously at dinner. Was this the son she had nursed at her bosom not so very long before? Surely he was developing rapidly.

81  "Well, Frank, I hope you can do that often," she said.

82  "I hope so, too, ma," was his rather noncommittal reply.

83  Auction sales were not to be discovered every day, however, and his home grocer was only open to one such transaction in a reasonable period of time, but from the very first young Cowperwood knew how to make money. He took subscriptions for a boys' paper, handled the agency for the sale of a new kind of ice-skate, and once organized a band of neighborhood youths into a union for the purpose of purchasing their summer straw hats at wholesale. It was not his idea that he could get rich by saving. From the first he had the notion that liberal spending was better, and that somehow he would get along.

84  It was in this year, or a little earlier, that he began to take an interest in girls. He had from the first a keen eye for the beautiful among them; and, being good-looking and magnetic himself, it was not difficult for him to attract the sympathetic interest of those in whom he was interested. A twelve-year-old girl, Patience Barlow, who lived further up the street, was the first to attract his attention or be attracted by him. Black hair and snapping black eyes were her portion, with pretty pigtails down her back, and dainty feet and ankles to match a dainty figure. She was a Quakeress, the daughter of Quaker parents, wearing a demure little bonnet. Her disposition, however, was vivacious, and she liked this self-reliant, self-sufficient, straight-spoken boy. One day, after an exchange of glances from time to time, he said, with a smile and the courage that was innate to him: "You live up my way, don't you?"

85  "Yes," she replied, a little flustered—this last manifested in a nervous swinging of her school-bag—"I live at number one-forty-one."

86  "I know the house," he said. "I've seen you go in there. You go to the same school my sister does, don't you? Aren't you Patience Barlow?" He had heard some of the boys speak her name.

87  "Yes. How do you know?"

88  "Oh, I've heard," he smiled. "I've seen you. Do you like licorice?"

89  He fished in his coat and pulled out some fresh sticks that were sold at the time.

90  "Thank you," she said, sweetly, taking one.

91 "It isn't very good. I've been carrying it a long time. I had some taffy the other day."

92 "Oh, it's all right," she replied, chewing the end of hers.

93 "Don't you know my sister, Anna Cowperwood?" he recurred, by way of self-introduction. "She's in a lower grade than you are, but I thought maybe you might have seen her."

94 "I think I know who she is. I've seen her coming home from school."

95 "I live right over there," he confided, pointing to his own home as he drew near to it, as if she didn't know. "I'll see you around here now, I guess."

96 "Do you know Ruth Merriam?" she asked, when he was about ready to turn off into the cobblestone road to reach his own door.

97 "No, why?"

98 "She's giving a party next Tuesday," she volunteered, seemingly pointlessly, but only seemingly.

99 "Where does she live?"

100 "There in twenty-eight."

101 "I'd like to go," he affirmed, warmly, as he swung away from her.

102 "Maybe she'll ask you," she called back, growing more courageous as the distance between them widened. "I'll ask her."

103 "Thanks," he smiled.

104 And she began to run gaily onward.

105 He looked after her with a smiling face. She was very pretty. He felt a keen desire to kiss her, and what might transpire at Ruth Merriam's party rose vividly before his eyes.

106 This was just one of the early love affairs, or puppy loves, that held his mind from time to time in the mixture of after events. Patience Barlow was kissed by him in secret ways many times before he found another girl. She and others of the street ran out to play in the snow of a winter's night, or lingered after dusk before her own door when the days grew dark early. It was so easy to catch and kiss her then, and to talk to her foolishly at parties.

107 Then came Dora Fitler, when he was sixteen years old and she was fourteen; and Marjorie Stafford, when he was seventeen and she was fifteen. Dora Fitler was a brunette, and Marjorie Stafford was as fair as the morning, with bright-red cheeks, bluish-gray eyes, and flaxen hair, and as plump as a partridge.

1. Which word best describes Frank Cowperwood's father's reaction to Frank's request for money?

    A. shocked
    B. doubtful
    C. unfair
    D. proud

2. Why can't Frank buy and sell groceries every day?

    A. He spends too much time with the boys' union.
    B. He would rather play with children his own age.
    C. He does not have the money to buy anything else.
    D. He cannot sell things to Mr. Dalrymple daily.

3. "Her disposition, however, was **vivacious**, and she liked this self-reliant, self-sufficient, straight-spoken boy."

    What does the word **vivacious** mean?

    A. vicious
    B. lively
    C. reserved
    D. greedy

4. Which word best describes Frank's attitude in this passage?

    A. confident
    B. hesitant
    C. gloomy
    D. disrespectful

5. "His plan was to have them carried on to his own home if the operation for any reason failed to go through. Though it was his first great venture, he was **cool as glass**."

   The author uses the phrase **cool as glass** to show that Frank is

   A. not fooling anyone
   B. deceiving someone
   C. calm and relaxed
   D. cunning and sly

6. Which statement represents what will most likely happen next in the passage?

   A. Mr. Dalrymple will only buy from Frank.
   B. Frank will grow up to be successful.
   C. The auctioneer will be mad at Frank.
   D. Frank will marry Marjorie one day.

7. Why is Frank most likely making rapid calculations in his head?

   A. He wonders whether or not his father will approve of the price.
   B. He is not sure that he has enough money to pay for the soap.
   C. He is figuring out how much the auctioneer is making.
   D. He wants to know if he can make money on the soap.

8. Which sentence from the passage most strongly develops a mood of curiosity?

   A. "Young Cowperwood was making a rapid calculation."
   B. "He drew nearer, his books tucked under his arm, and watched these operations closely."
   C. "Frank had bargained with him to deliver the soap for sixty cents."
   D. "From the first he had the notion that liberal spending was better, and that somehow he would get along."

9. Which word best describes Frank when he speaks with Patience Barlow?
    A. frightened
    B. dishonest
    C. charming
    D. uninterested

10. Identify and explain how Frank could have lost money on the deal that he made with Mr. Dalrymple. Use at least one detail from the passage to support your answer.

11. Describe a skill that you have learned to do well. Compare how you learned and have used this skill with Frank's experiences. Use information from the passage to support your answer.

# POISON IVY AND ITS COUSINS

1. The poison ivy plant is the bane of millions of campers, hikers, gardeners, and others who enjoy the great outdoors. So are its cousins: poison oak and poison sumac. Approximately 85 percent of the population will develop an allergic reaction if exposed to poison ivy, oak, or sumac. Usually, people develop a sensitivity to poison ivy, oak, or sumac only after several encounters with the plants. However, sensitivity may occur after only one exposure.

2. The cause of the rash, blisters, and infamous itch is "urushiol." It is a chemical in the sap of poison ivy, oak, and sumac plants. Because urushiol is inside the plant, brushing against an intact plant will not cause a reaction. But undamaged plants are rare. Stems or leaves broken by the wind or by animals and even the tiny holes made by chewing insects can release urushiol.

3. Reactions, treatments and preventive measures are the same for all three poison plants. Avoiding direct contact with the plants reduces the risk, but doesn't guarantee against a reaction. Urushiol can stick to pets, garden tools, balls, or anything it comes in contact with. If the urushiol isn't washed off those objects or animals, just touching them could cause a reaction in a susceptible person.

4. Urushiol that's rubbed off the plants onto other things can remain potent for years, depending on the environment. If the contaminated object is in a dry environment, the potency of the urushiol can last for decades. Even if the environment is warm and moist, the urushiol could still cause a reaction a year later.

5. Almost all parts of the body are vulnerable to the sticky urushiol. Because the chemical must penetrate the skin to cause a reaction, places where the skin is thick, such as the soles of the feet and the palms of the hands, are less sensitive to the sap than areas where the skin is thinner. The severity of the reaction may also depend on how large a dose of urushiol the person gets.

6. Urushiol can penetrate the skin within minutes. There is no time to waste if you know that you have been exposed. The earlier you cleanse the skin, the greater the chance that you can remove the urushiol before it gets through the skin. Cleansing may not stop the initial rash if more than ten minutes has elapsed. However, it can help prevent the rash from spreading further.

7. If you've been exposed to poison ivy, oak, or sumac, stay indoors until you complete the first two steps: Cleanse exposed skin with generous amounts of rubbing alcohol. Don't go near plants the same day. Alcohol removes your skin's protection as well as the urushiol. Any new contact will cause the urushiol to penetrate twice as fast.

1. The author most likely wrote this passage in order to

    A. explain which plants can be eaten
    B. inform readers about harmful plants
    C. persuade readers to travel outside
    D. describe cures for all kinds of injuries

2. "The poison ivy plant is the **bane** of millions of campers, hikers, gardeners, and others who enjoy the great outdoors."

    What does the word **bane** mean?

    A. creative spark
    B. source of comfort
    C. cause of harm
    D. reason for changes

3. Where does urushiol last the longest?

    A. in a dry environment
    B. on the forest floor
    C. on a person's skin
    D. in a cold environment

4. Why is cleaning with alcohol both helpful and dangerous? Use details from the passage to support your answer.

# JAMES P. BECKWOURTH, BLACK MOUNTAIN MAN

1. Trapping beaver and other animals for their fur in the early 1800s was a lonely and often dangerous way of life. Living under difficult conditions and forced to hunt daily for food, it was not a profession undertaken lightly. The privations were made up for with the chance to become rich in a short period of time. What few know, however, is that the fur trade empires created opportunities for people from many ethnic backgrounds. Trappers included Hawaiians, native New Mexicans, French Canadians, people of African ancestry, and eastern American Indians from the Shawnee, Delaware, and Iroquois tribes.

2. Of the black trappers making a living in the Rocky Mountains, none is as well known as James P. Beckwourth. He was born to Jennings Beckwith, a slaveowner, and a plantation slave named Miss Kill in Frederick County, Virginia around 1797.

3. One of several mixed-race siblings, young James Beckwith moved with his father to St. Louis, Missouri, in the early years of the 19th century. As a boy, he learned about his natural surroundings. He spent time hunting in the outskirts of French St. Louis. He apprenticed to a blacksmith. After a while, he ran away. Later, he became part of a trapping expedition on the Wood River.

4. Drawn to the outdoor life, Beckwith changed his name to Beckwourth. He joined the 1825 trapping party to the Rocky Mountains led by General William H. Ashley. The black mountain man claimed to have lived with the Blackfoot and later the Crow peoples. He learned the Crow language and married several Crow women. In 1825, Ashley made himself rich by reintroducing an American Indian idea. He brought goods and supplies to a prearranged place in the mountains. There he traded his goods for the trappers' pelts.

5. As a trapper for Ashley, Beckwourth rubbed shoulders with many of the famous trappers of his day. He was a contemporary of such men as Jim Bridger, Christopher "Kit" Carson, Tom "Broken Hand" Fitzpatrick, and Moses "Black" Harris. Beckwourth claimed to have been part of a group of trappers who established El Pueblo, a trading post on the Arkansas River that later became the city of Pueblo, Colorado.

6. Beckwourth found a freedom in the mountains that would not have been possible for a black man anywhere else in the United States at that time. Beckwourth worked as an independent trader and as an employee of Bent, St. Vrain and Co. at Bent's Old Fort and for the American Fur Company.

7. Beckwourth traveled to New Mexico where he opened a hotel and gambling parlor. From there he took dispatches to California for the U.S. military. He later moved to California during the "Gold Rush." There he set up a store. He also discovered a pass in the Sierra Nevada Mountains that is still called "Beckwourth Pass."

8   Beckwourth followed gold miners to Colorado in 1859. He was a part of the beginnings of Denver, Colorado. Always restless, Beckwourth traveled back and forth across the west until taking a job as an interpreter for the 1866 Carrington Expedition out of Fort Laramie, Wyoming.

9   Riding to Fort C.F. Smith in what is Montana today, Beckwourth complained of headaches and nosebleeds. He stopped in the camp of his old friends, the Crow. There Beckwourth suffered symptoms of a stroke. He died at sixty-seven or sixty-eight years of age. He was buried on Crow land in that same area near the present Bighorn Canyon National Recreation Area. James Beckwourth's final resting place was far from his Virginia birthplace, but fitting for this African-American adventurer.


1. Which word best describes the tone of the passage?

   A. humorous
   B. irritated
   C. secretive
   D. instructive


2. The author most likely included the information in the first paragraph of the passage to

   A. analyze the desire for fur
   B. describe trappers' lives
   C. introduce Beckwourth
   D. compare today to the past


3. "He was a **contemporary** of such men as Jim Bridger, Christopher 'Kit' Carson, Tom 'Broken Hand' Fitzpatrick, and Moses 'Black' Harris."

   What does the word **contemporary** mean?

   A. peer
   B. enemy
   C. hunter
   D. teacher

4. How did Beckwourth first learn to love the outdoors?

   A. by living among the Crow people
   B. by being raised by Miss Kill
   C. by meeting "Kit" Carson
   D. by hunting around St. Louis

5. Why do you think that James Beckwourth probably chose to live and die among the Crow? Use details from the passage to support your answer.

# AFRICAN AMERICANS IN COMBAT

1. "We officers of the Tenth Cavalry could have taken our black heroes into our arms. They had fought their way into our affections, as they have fought their way into the hearts of the American people." General John J. Pershing wrote these words. He was referring to the all-black 10th U.S. Cavalry that he had commanded during the battle of San Juan Hill, July 1, 1898.

2. General Pershing wrote the following words as well. They were part of a secret communiqué addressed to the French military stationed with the American army. It was dated August 7, 1918.

> We must prevent the rise of any pronounced degree of intimacy between French officers and Black officers. We may be courteous and amiable with the last but we cannot deal with them on the same plane as white American officers without deeply wounding the latter. We must not eat with them, must not shake hands with them, seek to talk to them or to meet with them outside the requirements of military service. We must not commend too highly these troops, especially in front of white Americans. Make a point of keeping the native cantonment from spoiling the Negro. White Americans become very incensed at any particular expression of intimacy between white women and black men.

3. Five months after General Pershing praised black fighting men at San Juan Hill, that same regiment was stationed in Huntsville, Alabama. There, a black civilian killed two black enlisted men. He had been apparently motivated by a belief that whites would pay a reward for every dead black soldier. This is an example of the confusion regarding the worth of the black soldier and sailor in American military service.

4. Blacks contributed to the defense of the colonies long before the American Revolution, but were excluded from the colonial militia in peacetime. In fact, there has been no U.S. war and few battles that have not involved Americans of African descent. They fought on both sides in the American Revolution. They have been in every war, declared or otherwise, from that time until the present.

5. Until 1948, the American military had always been segregated. In peacetime, the country—and the southern states in particular—were reluctant to arm blacks. And in war, the country generally allowed blacks to serve only after white recruitment shortages became an issue. In spite of that, African Americans often served honorably and fought hard overseas to win or preserve freedoms that they themselves did not enjoy at home.

6. The story of African Americans in combat is little different from the story of whites in the military. There have been heroes and there have been cowards. There has been competence and there has been ineptitude. However, there are two exceptions. There are two things that make the experience different. The first exception is that blacks have always had to deal with racism while proving that the stereotype of the unfit black warrior is false.

7    The second exception is that the black warriors have often been invisible to the public. Television and movies, from which so many Americans learn about history, have often glorified white heroes. Many shows have not even mentioned the roles played by black soldiers and sailors. In the popular 1970 movie, *Patton*, the main character is played by George C. Scott; General George S. Patton, Jr., gives a famous and memorable speech to a battalion of white soldiers. In fact, that famous speech was actually given to the all-black 761st Tank Battalion.

1. Which word best describes General Pershing in this passage?

    A. supportive
    B. dominant
    C. dishonest
    D. observant

2. The author most likely wrote this passage to

    A. tell readers about the adventures of an African-American soldier
    B. encourage readers to show their support for soldiers in the military
    C. explain how French soldiers and American soldiers got along
    D. show how African-American soldiers were often treated unfairly

3. Which information from the passage best represents the prejudice that African-American soldiers experienced?

    A. questions and answers
    B. quotes from Pershing
    C. reviews of old movies
    D. summaries of battles

# from "THE RED-HEADED LEAGUE"

*by Arthur Conan Doyle*

1     There was nothing in the office but a couple of wooden chairs and a deal table, behind which sat a small man, with a head that was even redder than mine. He said a few words to each candidate as he came up, and then he always managed to find some fault in them which would disqualify them. Getting a vacancy did not seem to be such a very easy matter after all. However, when our turn came, the little man was much more favorable to me than to any of the others, and he closed the door as we entered, so that he might have a private word with us.

2     "This is Mr. Jabez Wilson," said my assistant, "and he is willing to fill a vacancy in the League."

3     "And he is admirably suited for it," the other answered. "He has every requirement. I cannot recall when I have seen anything so fine." He took a step backward, cocked his head on one side, and gazed at my hair until I felt quite bashful. Then suddenly he plunged forward, wrung my hand, and congratulated me warmly on my success.

4     "It would be injustice to hesitate," said he. "You will, however, I am sure, excuse me for taking an obvious precaution." With that he seized my hair in both his hands, and tugged until I yelled with the pain. "There is water in your eyes," said he, as he released me. "I perceive that all is as it should be. But we have to be careful, for we have twice been deceived by wigs and once by paint. I could tell you tales of cobbler's wax which would disgust you with human nature." He stepped over to the window and shouted through it at the top of his voice that the vacancy was filled. A groan of disappointment came up from below, and the folk all trooped away in different directions, until there was not a red head to be seen except my own and that of the manager.

5     "My name," said he, "is Mr. Duncan Ross, and I am myself one of the pensioners upon the fund left by our noble benefactor. Are you a married man, Mr. Wilson? Have you a family?"

6     I answered that I had not.

7     His face fell immediately.

8     "Dear me!" he said, gravely, "that is very serious indeed! I am sorry to hear you say that. The fund was, of course, for the propagation and spread of the red heads as well as for their maintenance. It is exceedingly unfortunate that you should be a bachelor."

9     My face lengthened at this, Mr. Holmes, for I thought that I was not to have the vacancy after all; but, after thinking it over for a few minutes, he said that it would be all right.

10  "In the case of another," said he, "the objection might be fatal, but we must stretch a point in favor of a man with such a head of hair as yours. When shall you be able to enter upon your new duties?"

11  "Well, it is a little awkward, for I have a business already," said I.

12  "Oh, never mind about that, Mr. Wilson!" said Vincent Spaulding. "I shall be able to look after that for you."

13  "What would be the hours?" I asked.

14  "Ten to two."

15  Now a pawnbroker's business is mostly done of an evening, Mr. Holmes, especially Thursday and Friday evenings, which is just before pay day; so it would suit me very well to earn a little in the mornings. Besides, I knew that my assistant was a good man, and that he would see to anything that turned up.

16  "That would suit me very well," said I. "And the pay?"

17  "Is four pounds a week."

18  "And the work?"

19  "Is purely nominal."

20  "What do you call purely nominal?"

21  "Well, you have to be in the office, or at least in the building, the whole time. If you leave, you forfeit your whole position forever. The will is very clear upon that point. You don't comply with the conditions if you budge from the office during that time."

22  "It's only four hours a day, and I should not think of leaving," said I.

23  "No excuse will avail," said Mr. Duncan Ross, "neither sickness, nor business, nor anything else. There you must stay, or you lose your billet."

24  "And the work?"

25  "Is to copy out the 'Encyclopaedia Britannica.' There is the first volume of it in that press. You must find your own ink, pens, and blotting paper, but we provide this table and chair. Will you be ready tomorrow?"

26  "Certainly," I answered.

27  "Then, good-by, Mr. Jabez Wilson, and let me congratulate you once more on the important position which you have been fortunate enough to gain." He bowed me out

of the room, and I went home with my assistant hardly knowing what to say or do, I was so pleased at my own good fortune.

1. What is this story mostly about?

    A. why hair has different colors
    B. how encyclopedias are useful
    C. a man worrying about his hair
    D. a man starting an unusual job

2. Why was Jabez Wilson considered perfect for the job?

    A. He had a head full of red hair.
    B. He was a friend of Duncan Ross.
    C. He did not have a large family.
    D. He had spoken to Mr. Holmes.

3. "And the work?"

    "Is **purely nominal**."

    What does the speaker mean when he says the work is **purely nominal**?

    A. The job was meant for one special man.
    B. He did not want people to know about the job.
    C. He felt that the job was a suspicious affair.
    D. The job did not require very much effort.

4. "'I **perceive** that all is as it should be.'"

    What does the word **perceive** mean?

    A. fear
    B. expect
    C. sense
    D. tolerate

5. Based on the information in this story, what do you think the purpose of the Red-Headed League might have been? Use details from the story to support your answer.

# THE QUEST FOR HAPPINESS

### from "DELICATESSEN"
### *by Joyce Kilmer*

Here is a shop of wonderment.
From every land has come a prize;
Rich spices from the Orient,
And fruit that knew Italian skies,

And figs that ripened by the sea
In Smyrna, nuts from hot Brazil,
Strange pungent meats from
    Germany,
And currants from a Grecian hill.

He is the lord of goodly things
That make the poor man's table gay,
Yet of his worth no minstrel sings
And on his tomb there is no bay.

Perhaps he lives and dies unpraised,
This trafficker in humble sweets,
Because his little shops are raised
By thousands in the city streets.

Yet stars in greater numbers shine,
And violets in millions grow,
And they in many a golden line
Are sung, as every child must know.
Perhaps Fame thinks his worried
    eyes,
His wrinkled, shrewd, pathetic face,
His shop, and all he sells and buys,
Are desperately commonplace.

Well, it is true he has no sword
To dangle at his booted knees.
He leans across a slab of board,
And draws his knife and slices cheese.

He never heard of chivalry,
He longs for no heroic times;
He thinks of pickles, olives, tea,
And dollars, nickels, cents and dimes.

His world has narrow walls, it seems;
By counters is his soul confined;
His wares are all his hopes and
    dreams,
They are the fabric of his mind.

Yet—in a room above the store
There is a woman—and a child
Pattered just now across the floor;
The shopman looked at him and
    smiled.

For, once he thrilled with high
    romance
And tuned to love his eager voice.
Like any cavalier of France
He wooed the maiden of his choice.

And now deep in his weary heart
Are sacred flames that whitely burn.
He has of Heaven's grace a part
Who loves, who is beloved in turn.

And when the long day's work is done,
(How slow the leaden minutes ran!)
Home, with his wife and little son,
He is no huckster, but a man!

He decks his window artfully,
He haggles over paltry sums.
In this strange field his war must be
And by such blows his triumph comes.

What if no trumpet sounds to call
His armed legions to his side?
What if, to no ancestral hall
He comes in all a victor's pride?

This man has home and child and
    wife
And battle set for every day.
This man has God and love and life;
These stand, all else shall pass away.

## "YOUNG LOCHINVAR"
### *by Sir Walter Scott*

Oh young Lochinvar is come out of the west,
Through all the wide Border his steed was the best;
And save his good broadsword he weapon had none;
He rode all unarm'd, and he rode all alone.
So faithful in love, and so dauntless in war,
There never was knight like the young Lochinvar.

He staid not for brake, and he stopp'd not for stone,
He swam the Esk river where ford there was none;
But ere he alighted at Netherby gate,
The bride had consented, the gallant came late:
For a laggard in love, and a dastard in war,
Was to wed the fair Ellen of brave Lochinvar.

So boldly he enter'd the Netherby Hall,
Among brid'smen, and kinsmen, and brothers, and all;
Then spoke the bride's father, his hand on his sword,
(For the poor craven bridegroom said never a word,)
"O come ye in peace here, or come ye in war,
Or to dance at our bridal, young Lord Lochinvar?"—

"I long woo'd your daughter, my suit you denied;—
Love swells like the Solway, but ebbs like its tide—
And now am I come, with this lost love of mine,
To lead but one measure, drink one cup of wine.
There are maidens in Scotland more lovely by far,
That would gladly be bride to the young Lochinvar."

The bride kiss'd the goblet; the knight took it up,
He quaff'd off the wine, and he threw down the cup.
She look'd down to blush, and she look'd up to sigh,
With a smile on her lips, and a tear in her eye.
He took her soft hand, ere her mother could bar,—
"Now tread we a measure!" said young Lochinvar.

So stately his form, and so lovely her face,
That never a hall such a galliard did grace;
While her mother did fret, and her father did fume,
And the bridegroom stood dangling his bonnet and plume;
And the bride-maidens whispered, " 'T were better by far,
To have match'd our fair cousin with young Lochinvar."

One touch to her hand, and one word in her ear,
When they reach'd the hall-door, and the charger stood near;
So light to the croupe the fair lady he swung,
So light to the saddle before her he sprung!

"She is won! we are gone, over bank, bush, and scaur;
They'll have fleet steeds that follow," quoth young Lochinvar.

There was mounting 'mong Græmes of the Netherby clan;
Forsters, Fenwicks, and Musgraves, they rode and they ran:
There was racing and chasing on Cannobie Lea,
But the lost bride of Netherby ne'er did they see.
So daring in love, and so dauntless in war,
Have ye e'er heard of gallant like young Lochinvar?

1. The author most likely wrote the first poem to

   A. explain why readers should become shopkeepers
   B. compare many kinds of commonplace tasks
   C. show how a shopkeeper can be as heroic as a soldier
   D. describe what it might be like to be a soldier

2. Which lines from the first poem best represent the importance of the shopkeeper's job?

   A. "Well, it is true he has no sword / To dangle at his booted knee."
   B. "He is the lord of goodly things / That make the poor man's table gay."
   C. "For, once he thrilled with high romance / And tuned to love his eager voice."
   D. "What if no trumpet sounds to call / His armed legions to his side?"

3. In the first poem, what does the shopkeeper fight for?

   A. fame
   B. his country
   C. survival
   D. more money

4. The shopkeeper in the first poem thinks that what is most important is

   A. his store
   B. soldiers
   C. adventure
   D. his family


5. Which theme applies best to the second poem?

   A. Never leave the ones you love.
   B. Go after what you want.
   C. All people are good in some way.
   D. Be careful what you wish for.


6. "While her mother did fret, and her father did fume, / And the bridegroom **stood dangling his bonnet and plume**;"

   The author uses the phrase **stood dangling his bonnet and plume** to show that the bridegroom

   A. is unaware of what is happening.
   B. is not going to stand up for himself.
   C. thinks that he is dressed very well.
   D. worries that the others are bored.


7. How did the bride-maidens feel about Lochinvar?

   A. They thought that he was good for the bride.
   B. They thought that he was brave for coming to the wedding.
   C. They thought that he was rude when he visited.
   D. They thought that he should learn from the bridegroom.

8. Lochinvar wanted to dance with the bride in order to

    A. make the bride's father fume.
    B. make the two of them appear to be good friends.
    C. apologize for leaving the bride.
    D. give the couple a chance to escape.

9. How are the two poems alike?

    A. Both are about famous adventurers.
    B. Both are about depressed people.
    C. Both present men who are pursuing goals.
    D. Both deal with exotic faraway lands.

10. Why does the speaker of the first poem believe the delicatessen owner is worth writing about? Use details from the passage to support your answer.

11. Why did Lochinvar most likely wait so long before stealing Ellen away? Use details from the passage to support your answer.

# "GET UP AND BAR THE DOOR"

### I.

IT fell about the Martinmas time,
And a gay time it was then,
When our goodwife got puddings to make,
And she's boil'd them in the pan.

### II.

The wind sae cauld blew south and north,
And blew into the floor;
Quoth our goodman to our goodwife,
'Gae out and bar the door.'—

### III.

'My hand is in my hussyfskap,
Goodman, as ye may see;
An' it shou'dna be barr'd this hundred year,
It 's no be barr'd for me.'—

### IV.

They made a paction 'tween them twa,
They made it firm and sure,
That the first word whae'er shou'd speak,
Shou'd rise and bar the door.

### V.

Then by there came two gentlemen,
At twelve o' clock at night,
And they could neither see house nor hall,
Nor coal nor candle-light.

### VI.

Now whether is this a rich man's house,
Or whether is it a poor?'
But ne'er a word wad ane o' them speak,
For barring of the door.

### VII.

And first they ate the white puddings,
And then they ate the black.
Tho' muckle thought the goodwife to hersel'
Yet ne'er a word she spake.

### VIII.

Then said the one unto the other,
'Here, man, tak ye my knife;
Do ye tak aff the auld man's beard,
And I'll kiss the goodwife.'—

### IX.

'But there's nae water in the house,
And what shall we do than?'—
'What ails ye at the pudding-broo,
That boils into the pan?'

### X.

O up then started our goodman,
An angry man was he:
'Will ye kiss my wife before my een,
And sca'd me wi' pudding-bree?'

### XI.

Then up and started our goodwife,
Gied three skips on the floor:
'Goodman, you've spoken the foremost word!
Get up and bar the door.'

1. The author most likely wrote this poem to

   A. explain why people should always lock their doors.
   B. show what can happen when married couples argue.
   C. illustrate how life can be dangerous in wintertime.
   D. tell an amusing story about an unusual couple.

2. Which word best describes both the husband and wife in the passage?

   A. ambitious
   B. helpful
   C. stubborn
   D. bashful

3. What are the first three stanzas mostly about?

   A. a wife who wants her husband to close the door
   B. a husband who wants his wife to make pudding
   C. two people who argue about locking the door
   D. two people who try to forget that winter has come

4. Why did the man want his wife to close the door?

   A. A cold wind was blowing inside.
   B. It would soon be midnight.
   C. People were coming to visit.
   D. He was embarrassed about his house.

5. Why did the wife refuse to close the door?

   A. She wanted to meet new people.
   B. She thought that the door didn't close.
   C. She was afraid of the cold wind.
   D. She was busy making pudding.

6. What kinds of men arrived at midnight?

   A. soldiers
   B. old friends
   C. mean bullies
   D. tourists

7. Why did the husband most likely speak up?

    A. He was hungry for black and white pudding.
    B. He was startled by the unexpected visitors.
    C. He was furious about what was happening.
    D. He was finally ready to go and close the door.

8. What is the purpose of the unusual spellings in the poem?

    A. to show the way that people once spoke
    B. to suggest that the husband was smart
    C. to suggest that the wife was deceitful
    D. to show that the couple was very old

# "THE MEN THAT DON'T FIT IN"
*by Robert W. Service*

There's a race of men that don't fit in,
A race that can't stay still;
So they break the hearts of kith and kin,
And they roam the world at will.
They range the field and they rove the flood,
And they climb the mountain's crest;
Theirs is the curse of the gypsy blood,
And they don't know how to rest.

If they just went straight they might go far;
They are strong and brave and true;
But they're always tired of the things that are,
And they want the strange and new.
They say: "Could I find my proper groove,
What a deep mark I would make!"
So they chop and change, and each fresh move
Is only a fresh mistake.

And each forgets, as he strips and runs
With a brilliant, fitful pace,
It's the steady, quiet, plodding ones
Who win in the lifelong race.
And each forgets that his youth has fled,
Forgets that his prime is past,
Till he stands one day, with a hope that's dead,
In the glare of the truth at last.

He has failed, he has failed; he has missed his chance;
He has just done things by half.
Life's been a jolly good joke on him,
And now is the time to laugh.
Ha, ha! He is one of the Legion Lost;
He was never meant to win;
He's a rolling stone, and it's bred in the bone;
He's a man who won't fit in.

> 1　**Robert Service** was born in Preston, Lancashire, England. His parents were Scottish. He spent his childhood in Scotland. He attended the University of Glasgow. His vagabond career took him throughout the world. He worked at a wide variety of jobs, from cook to clerk, from hobo to correspondent. He emigrated to Canada in 1894. He took a job with the Canadian Bank of Commerce. He was stationed for eight years in Whitehorse, Yukon. It was while in the Yukon that he published his first book of poems, *Songs of a Sourdough*. It was to make him famous.
>
> 2　Writing became a career. He was a correspondent for *The Toronto Star* during the Balkan Wars of 1912–1913. He was an ambulance driver and correspondent in France during World War I. He settled in France after World War I and married a French woman.

1. How does the speaker most likely feel about the men in this poem?

   A. motivated
   B. supported
   C. flustered
   D. saddened

2. What is this poem mostly about?

   A. men who can't escape their pasts
   B. the history of the Legion Lost
   C. restless and unsettled men
   D. a way for people to fix their lives

3. "So they break the hearts of **kith and kin**,"

   The phrase **kith and kin** is an example of

   A. personification
   B. alliteration
   C. metaphor
   D. onomatopoeia

4. Think about how the poet describes the men in the poem. Which does the poet think is best—a steady, quiet, plodding life, or a wild, wandering, adventurous life? Use details from the passage to support your answer.

1   **Harriet Beecher Stowe** was born June 14, 1811, in Litchfield, Connecticut. Her father, the Reverend Lyman Beecher (1775–1863), was a prominent Congregational minister. Harriet was a student at Hartford Female Seminary. The school had been founded by her sister, Catharine. Harriet later taught there.

2   In 1832, Harriet moved with her family to Cincinnati, Ohio. Her father became president of Lane Theological Seminary. In Cincinnati, Harriet married Calvin E. Stowe. He was a professor at Lane. Cincinnati was just across the river from Kentucky. Kentucky was a slave state. It was in Cincinnati that Harriet first became aware of the horrors of slavery.

3   Harriet and Calvin learned that their servant, Zillah, was actually a runaway slave. Calvin and Henry Ward Beecher drove her to the next station on the Underground Railroad. One night, Harriet's friend, Mr. Rankin, saw a young woman run across the Ohio River. It was winter. She was able to cross over the ice. She did it with a baby in her arms. This story moved Harriet deeply. It would later become one of the most famous scenes in *Uncle Tom's Cabin*.

4   In 1850, Professor Stowe joined the faculty of Bowdoin College. It was located in Brunswick, Maine. The Stowe family moved to Maine. They lived in Brunswick until 1853. In Brunswick, Harriet wrote her great book, *Uncle Tom's Cabin*. In it she dramatized the horrors of slavery. It was more intense and moving than all the abolitionist literature. The book was a great success. It changed the minds of a huge part of the population.

5   Abraham Lincoln met Harriet Beecher Stowe in 1862. He said, "So you're the little woman who wrote the book that started this Great War!"

# "HARRIET BEECHER STOWE"
*by Paul Laurence Dunbar*

SHE told the story, and the whole world wept
At wrongs and cruelties it had not known
But for this fearless woman's voice alone.
She spoke to consciences that long had slept:
Her message, Freedom's clear reveille, swept
From heedless hovel to complacent throne.
Command and prophecy were in the tone,
And from its sheath the sword of justice leapt.
Around two peoples swelled a fiery wave,
But both came forth transfigured from the flame.
Blest be the hand that dared be strong to save,
And blest be she who in our weakness came—
Prophet and priestess! At one stroke she gave
A race to freedom and herself to fame.

1. The author most likely wrote this poem to

   A. honor Stowe for her accomplishments
   B. explain the history of slavery in America
   C. compare great works written on slavery
   D. review the story of *Uncle Tom's Cabin*


2. "From heedless hovel to **complacent** throne."

   What does the word **complacent** mean?

   A. poor and wretched
   B. triumphant
   C. smug and at ease
   D. luxurious


3. Which of the following states how Harriet Beecher Stowe felt about slavery?

   A. It was a benefit to the nation.
   B. It was a necessary social evil.
   C. It was a southern tradition.
   D. It was a great injustice.


4. Why was the woman running across the ice?

   A. She was fleeing from slavery to freedom.
   B. She was looking for a doctor for her baby.
   C. She was bringing her baby to her family.
   D. She was searching for Harriet Beecher Stowe.

5. Do Abraham Lincoln and Paul Laurence Dunbar agree about Harriet Beecher Stowe? Use details from the passage to support your answer.

# Excerpted from "THE PIED PIPER OF HAMELIN, A CHILD'S STORY"

*by Robert Browning*

### I.

Hamelin Town's in Brunswick,
By famous Hanover city;
The river Weser, deep and wide,
Washes its wall on the southern side
A pleasanter spot you never spied;
But, when begins my ditty,
Almost five hundred years ago,
To see the townsfolk suffer so
From vermin, was a pity.

### II.

Rats!
They fought the dogs and killed the cats,
And bit the babies in the cradles,
And ate the cheeses out of the vats,
And licked the soup from the cook's own ladles.
Split open the kegs of salted sprats,
Made nests inside men's Sunday hats,
And even spoiled the women's chats
By drowning their speaking
With shrieking and squeaking
In fifty different sharps and flats.

### III.

At last the people in a body
To the Town Hall came flocking:
" 'Tis clear," cried they, "our Mayor's a noddy;
And as for our Corporation—shocking
To think we buy gowns lined with ermine
For dolts that can't or won't determine
What's best to rid us of our vermin!
Rouse up, sirs! Give your brains a racking
To find the remedy we're lacking,
Or, sure as fate, we'll send you packing!"
At this the Mayor and Corporation
Quaked with a mighty consternation.

### IV.

"Bless us," cried the Mayor, "what's that?"
(With the Corporation as he sat
Looking little though wondrous fat;
Nor brighter was his eye, nor moister
Than a too-long-opened oyster,
Save when at noon his paunch grew mutinous
For a plate of turtle green and glutinous),
"Only a scraping of shoes on the mat
Anything like the sound of a rat
Makes my heart go pit-a-pat!"

### V.

"Come in!"—the Mayor cried, looking bigger:
And in did come the strangest figure!
His queer long coat from heel to head
Was half of yellow and half of red,
And he himself was tall and thin,
With sharp blue eyes, each like a pin,
And light loose hair, yet swarthy skin,
No tuft on cheek nor beard on chin,
But lips where smiles went out and in;
There was no guessing his kith and kin:

And nobody could enough admire
The tall man and his quaint attire.

### VI.

He advanced to the council-table:
And, "Please your honors," said he, "I'm able,
By means of a secret charm, to draw
All creatures living beneath the sun,
That creep or swim or fly or run,
After me so as you never saw!
And I chiefly use my charm
On creatures that do people harm,
The mole and toad and newt and viper;
And people call me the Pied Piper."
(And here they noticed round his neck
A scarf of red and yellow stripe,
To match with his coat of the self-same cheque;
And at the scarf's end hung a pipe;
And his fingers, they noticed, were ever straying
As if impatient to be playing
Upon this pipe, as low it dangled
Over his vesture so old-fangled.)
"Yet," said he, "poor piper as I am,
In Tartary I freed the Cham,
Last June, from his huge swarms of gnats;
I eased in Asia the Nizam
Of a monstrous brood of vampyre-bats:
And as for what your brain bewilders,
If I can rid your town of rats
Will you give me a thousand guilders?"
"One? fifty thousand!"—was the exclamation
Of the astonished Mayor and Corporation.

1. What is this passage mostly about?

    A. how mayors run towns
    B. the dangers of rats
    C. a man who arrives in town
    D. the advisors to a mayor

2. Which word best describes the Mayor?

    A. reserved
    B. devoted
    C. focused
    D. worried

3. "And I chiefly use my charm / On creatures that do people harm, / The mole and toad and newt and viper; / And people call me the Pied Piper."

   The Pied Piper identifies himself as a person who

   A. uses his power to get rid of pests.
   B. uses his power to take over towns.
   C. wants to be in the Corporation.
   D. hopes to learn more about animals.

4. " 'One? fifty thousand!'—was the exclamation / Of the astonished Mayor and Corporation."

   The Mayor's words show that he is

   A. familiar with the Pied Piper's work.
   B. desperate to get rid of the rats.
   C. outraged by the Pied Piper's demands.
   D. not concerned with the people.

5. Which words best describe the Pied Piper?

   A. mean and scary
   B. active and colorful
   C. pushy and forceful
   D. caring and generous

6. Why did people complain about the Mayor?

   A. He had allowed the Pied Piper into town.
   B. He had done nothing about the rat crisis.
   C. He ate too much and left nothing for them.
   D. He did not encourage his staff to do work.

7. What do you think will happen next? Use details from the passage to support your answer.

# from "HIAWATHA'S CHILDHOOD"
## by Henry Wadsworth Longfellow

By the shores of Gitche Gumee,
By the shining Big-Sea-Water,
Stood the wigwam of Nokomis,
Daughter of the moon, Nokomis.
Dark behind it rose the forest,
Rose the black and gloomy pine
   trees,
Rose the firs with cones upon them.
Bright before it beat the water,
Beat the clear and sunny water,
Beat the shining Big-Sea-Water.

There the wrinkled old Nokomis
Nursed the little Hiawatha,
Rocked him in his linden cradle,
Bedded soft in moss and rushes,
Safely bound with reindeer sinews;
Stilled his fretful wail by saying,
"Hush! the Naked Bear will hear
   thee!"
Lulled him into slumber, singing,
"Ewa-yea! my little owlet!
Who is this that lights the wigwam?
With his great eyes lights the
   wigwam?
Ewa-yea! my little owlet!"

Many things Nokomis taught him
Of the stars that shine in heaven;
Showed him Ishkoodah, the comet,
Ishkoodah with fiery tresses;
Showed the Death-Dance of the
   spirits,
Warriors with their plumes and war
   clubs,
Flaring far away to northward
In the frosty nights of winter;
Showed the broad white road in
   heaven,
Pathway of the ghosts, the shadows,
Running straight across the
   heavens,
Crowded with the ghosts, the
   shadows.

At the door on summer evenings
Sat the little Hiawatha;
Heard the whispering of the pine
   trees,
Heard the lapping of the waters,
Sounds of music, words of wonder;
"Minne-wawa" said the pine trees,
"Mudway-ashka!" said the water.

Saw the firefly, Wah-wah-taysee,
Flitting through the dusk of
   evening,
With the twinkle of its candle
Lighting up the brakes and bushes,
And he sang the song of children,
Sang the song Nokomis taught him:
"Wah-wah-taysee, little firefly,
Little, flitting, white-fire insect,
Little, dancing, white-fire creature,
Light me with your little candle,
Ere upon my bed I lay me,
Ere in sleep I close my eyelids!"

Saw the moon rise from the water,
Rippling, rounding from the water,
Saw the flecks and shadows on it,
Whispered, "What is that,
   Nokomis?"
And the good Nokomis answered:
"Once a warrior, very angry,
Seized his grandmother and threw
   her
Up into the sky at midnight;
Right against the moon he threw
   her.
'Tis her body that you see there."

Saw the rainbow in the heaven,
In the eastern sky, the rainbow,
Whispered, "What is that,
   Nokomis?"
And the good Nokomis answered:
" 'Tis the heaven of flowers you see
   there;

All the wild flowers of the forest,
All the lilies of the prairie,
When on earth they fade and perish,
Blossom in that heaven above us."

When he heard the owls at midnight,
Hooting, laughing, in the forest,
"What is that?" he cried in terror,
"What is that," he said, "Nokomis?"
And the good Nokomis answered.
"That is but the owl and owlet,
Talking in their native language,
Talking, scolding, at each other."

Then the little Hiawatha
Learned of every bird its language,
Learned their names and all their secrets,
How they built their nests in summer,
Where they hid themselves in winter,
Talked with them whene'er he met them,
Called them "Hiawatha's Chickens."

Of all beasts he learned the language,
Learned their names and all their secrets,
How the beavers built their lodges.
Where the squirrels hid their acorns,
How the reindeer ran so swiftly,
Why the rabbit was so timid,
Talked with them whene'er he met them,
Called them "Hiawatha's Brothers."

Then Iagoo the great boaster,
He the marvelous story-teller,
He the traveler and the talker,
He the friend of old Nokomis,
Made a bow for Hiawatha;
From a branch of ash he made it,
From an oak bough made the arrows,
Tipped with flint, and winged with feathers,
And the cord he made of deerskin.

Then he said to Hiawatha:
"Go, my son, into the forest,
Where the red deer herd together,
Kill for us a famous roebuck,
Kill for us a deer with antlers!"

Forth into the forest straightway
All alone walked Hiawatha
Proudly, with his bow and arrows;
And the birds sang round him, o'er him
"Do not shoot us, Hiawatha!"
Sang the robin, sang the bluebird,
"Do not shoot us, Hiawatha!"

And the rabbit from his pathway
Leaped aside, and at a distance
Sat erect upon his haunches,
Half in fear and half in frolic,
Saying to the little hunter,
"Do not shoot me, Hiawatha!"

But he heeded not, nor heard them,
For his thoughts were with the red deer;
On their tracks his eyes were fastened,
Leading downward to the river,
To the ford across the river,
And as one in slumber walked he.

Hidden in the alder bushes,
There he waited till the deer came,
Till he saw two antlers lifted,
Saw two eyes look from the thicket,
Saw two nostrils point to windward,
And a deer came down the pathway,
Flecked with leafy light and shadow.
And his heart within him fluttered
Trembled like the leaves above him,
Like the birch-leaf palpitated,
As the deer came down the pathway.

Then, upon one knee uprising,
Hiawatha aimed an arrow;
Scarce a twig moved with his motion,
Scarce a leaf was stirred or rustled,
But the wary roebuck darted,
Stamped with all his hoofs together,
Listened with one foot uplifted,
Leaped as if to meet the arrow;
Ah! the singing, fatal arrow,
Like a wasp it buzzed, and stung him!

Dead he lay there in the forest,
By the ford across the river;
Beat his timid heart no longer;
But the heart of Hiawatha
Throbbed and shouted and exulted,
As he bore the red deer homeward.

1. Which word best describes Hiawatha?

    A. mature
    B. unfriendly
    C. rebellious
    D. curious

2. Hiawatha is scared of the

    A. fireflies
    B. owls
    C. roebuck
    D. moon

3. Which tone is created through the author's word choices?

    A. frightened
    B. tragic
    C. grave
    D. respectful

4. " . . . the heart of Hiawatha / Throbbed and shouted and **exulted** . . . "

    What does the word **exulted** mean?

    A. growled
    B. wept
    C. rejoiced
    D. laughed

5. What does Nokomis think rainbows are?

    A. places where flowers go when they wilt
    B. spaces where the forest animals sleep
    C. reflections of the fireflies
    D. sunshine on the water

6. The author would probably agree that Nokomis taught Hiawatha to

    A. respect the animals
    B. make his own rainbows
    C. hunt with newer arrows
    D. chase away the fireflies

7. What were three of the lessons Nokomis taught Hiawatha? Use details from the passage to support your answer.

# from "THE RIME OF THE ANCIENT MARINER"
## by Samuel Taylor Coleridge

**PART I**

*An ancient Mariner meeteth three Gallants bidden to a wedding-feast, and detaineth one.*

It is an ancient Mariner,
And he stoppeth one of three.
'By thy long beard and glittering eye,
Now wherefore stopp'st thou me?

The Bridegroom's doors are opened wide,
And I am next of kin;
The guests are met, the feast is set:
May'st hear the merry din.'

He holds him with his skinny hand,
'There was a ship,' quoth he.
'Hold off! unhand me, grey-beard loon!'
Eftsoons his hand dropt he.

*The Wedding-Guest is spell-bound by the eye of the old seafaring man, and constrained to hear his tale.*

He holds him with his glittering eye—
The Wedding-Guest stood still,
And listens like a three years' child:
The Mariner hath his will.

The Wedding-Guest sat on a stone:
He cannot choose but hear;
And thus spake on that ancient man,
The bright-eyed Mariner.

The ship was cheered, the harbour cleared,
Merrily did we drop
Below the kirk, below the hill,
Below the lighthouse top.

*The Mariner tells how the ship sailed southward with a good wind and fair weather, till it reached the Line.*

The Sun came up upon the left,
Out of the sea came he!
And he shone bright, and on the right
Went down into the sea.

Higher and higher every day,
Till over the mast at noon—'
The Wedding-Guest here beat his breast,
For he heard the loud bassoon.

*The Wedding-Guest heareth the bridal music; but the Mariner continueth his tale.*

The bride hath paced into the hall,
Red as a rose is she;
Nodding their heads before her goes
The merry minstrelsy.

The Wedding-Guest he beat his breast,
Yet he cannot choose but hear;
And thus spake on that ancient man,
The bright-eyed Mariner.

*The ship driven by a storm toward the South Pole.*

'And now the STORM-BLAST came, and he
Was tyrannous and strong:
He struck with his o'ertaking wings,
And chased us south along.

With sloping masts and dipping prow,
As who pursued with yell and blow
Still treads the shadow of his foe,

And forward bends his head,
The ship drove fast, loud roared the blast,
The southward aye we fled.

And now there came both mist and snow,
And it grew wondrous cold:
And ice, mast-high, came floating by,
As green as emerald.

*The land of ice, and of fearful sounds where no living thing was to be seen.*

And through the drifts the snowy clifts
Did send a dismal sheen:
Nor shapes of men nor beasts we ken—
The ice was all between.

The ice was here, the ice was there,
The ice was all around:
It cracked and growled, and roared and howled,
Like noises in a swound!

*Till a great sea-bird, called the Albatross, came through the snow-fog, and was received with great joy and hospitality.*

At length did cross an Albatross,
Through the fog it came;
As if it had been a Christian soul,
We hailed it in God's name.

It ate the food it ne'er had eat,
And round and round it flew.
The ice did split with a thunder-fit;
The helmsman steered us through!

*And lo! the Albatross proveth a bird of good omen, and followeth the ship as it returned northward through fog and floating ice.*

And a good south wind sprung up behind;
The Albatross did follow,
And every day, for food or play,
Came to the mariner's hollo!

In mist or cloud, on mast or shroud,
It perched for vespers nine;
Whiles all the night, through fog-smoke white,
Glimmered the white Moon-shine.'

*The ancient Mariner inhospitably killeth the pious bird of good omen.*

'God save thee, ancient Mariner!
From the fiends, that plague thee thus!—
Why look'st thou so?'—With my crossbow
I shot the ALBATROSS.

## PART II

The Sun now rose upon the right:
Out of the sea came he,
Still hid in mist, and on the left
Went down into the sea.

And the good south wind still blew behind,
But no sweet bird did follow,
Nor any day for food or play
Came to the mariners' hollo!

*His shipmates cry out against the ancient Mariner, for killing the bird of good luck.*

And I had done an hellish thing,
And it would work 'em woe:
For all averred, I had killed the bird
That made the breeze to blow.

Ah wretch! said they, the bird to slay,
That made the breeze to blow!

*But when the fog cleared off, they justify the same, and thus make themselves accomplices in the crime.*

Nor dim nor red, like God's own head,
The glorious Sun uprist :
Then all averred, I had killed the bird
That brought the fog and mist.
'Twas right, said they, such birds to slay,
That bring the fog and mist.

*The fair breeze continues; the ship enters the Pacific Ocean, and sails northward, even till it reaches the Line.*

The fair breeze blew, the white foam flew,
The furrow followed free;
We were the first that ever burst
Into that silent sea.

*The ship hath been suddenly becalmed.*

Down dropt the breeze, the sails dropt down,
'Twas sad as sad could be;
And we did speak only to break
The silence of the sea!

All in a hot and copper sky,
The bloody Sun, at noon,
Right up above the mast did stand,
No bigger than the Moon.

Day after day, day after day,
We stuck, nor breath nor motion;
As idle as a painted ship
Upon a painted ocean.

*And the Albatross begins to be avenged.*

Water, water, every where,
And all the boards did shrink;
Water, water, every where,
Nor any drop to drink.

The very deep did rot: O Christ!
That ever this should be!
Yea, slimy things did crawl with legs
Upon the slimy sea.

About, about, in reel and rout
The death-fires danced at night;
The water, like a witch's oils,
Burnt green, and blue and white.

1. Why did the ship stop moving?

    A. The sailors did not want to leave.
    B. The water was not deep enough.
    C. The ship ran aground.
    D. The wind stopped pushing the sails.

2. "God save thee, ancient Mariner! / From the fiends, that **plague** thee . . ."

    What does the word **plague** mean?

    A. watch
    B. haunt
    C. assist
    D. gather

3. When the sun is over the mast at noon, what have the sailors reached?

    A. the North Pole
    B. the equator
    C. Great Britain
    D. the South Pole

4. "The Wedding-Guest stood still, / And **listens like a three years' child**:"

    The phrase **listens like a three years' child** is an example of

    A. hyperbole.
    B. irony.
    C. simile.
    D. assonance.

5. Why did the Wedding Guest beat his breast?

   A. He could not bear to leave the Ancient Mariner.
   B. He was frightened by seeing the Ancient Mariner.
   C. He did not like the music playing at the wedding.
   D. He wanted the bride to know that he was outside.

6. Which word best describes the speaker at the end of the poem?

   A. despairing
   B. angry
   C. impatient
   D. unconcerned

7. Why does the author most likely add some sections in italics?

   A. to show the wedding guest's speech
   B. to correct the Ancient Mariner's claims
   C. to help the reader understand the story
   D. to show that the events never happened

8. What happens to the ship and sailors at the end of this poem? Use details from the passage to support your answer.

# "TWO MOODS FROM THE HILL"
*by Ernest Benshimol*

### I. YOUTH

I LOVE to watch the world from here, for all
The numberless living portraits that are drawn
Upon the mind. Far over is the sea,
Fronting the sand, a few great yellow dunes,
A salt marsh stumbling after, rank and green,
With brackish gullies wandering in between,
All this from the hill.
And more: a clump of dwarfed and twisted cedars,
Sentinels over the marsh, and bright with the sun
A field of daisies wandering in the wind
As though a hidden serpent glided through,
A broken wall, a new-plowed field, and then
The dusty road and the abodes of men
Surrounding the hill.
How small the enclosure is wherein there lives
Each phase and passion of life, the distant sail
Dips in the limpid bosom of the sea,
From that far place to where in state the turf
Raises a throne for me upon the hill,
Each little love and lust of a living thing
Can thus be compassed in a rainbow ring
And seen from the hill.

### II. AGE

Why did I build my cottage on a hill
Facing the sea?
Why did I plan each terraced lawn to slope
Down to the deep blue billowy breast of hope,
Surging and sweeping,
laughing and leaping,
Tumbling its garments of foam upon the shore,
Rustling the sands that know my step no more,
I should have found a valley, deep and still,
To shelter me.

There flows the river, and it seems asleep
So far away,
Yet I remember whip of wave and roar
Of wind that rose and smote against the oar,
Smote and retreated,
Proud but defeated,
While I rejoiced and rowed into the brine,

Drawing on wet and heavy-straining line
The great cod quivering from the deep
As counterplay.

What is the solace of these hills and vales
That rise and fall?
What is there glorious in the greenwood glen,
Or twittering thrush or wing of darting wren?
Give me the gusty,
Raucous and rusty
Call of the sea gull in the echoing sky,
The wild shriek of the winds that cannot die,
Give me the life that follows the bending sails,
Or none at all!

1. Which statement best represents the attitude of the speaker in "Youth"?

    A. He felt afraid of the sea and would never want to venture there.
    B. He was interested in the sea only as part of the background.
    C. He was completely unaware of the sea; his attention was elsewhere.
    D. He loved the sea very much and was fascinated by every aspect of it.

2. "What is the **solace** of these hills and vales / That rise and fall?"

    What does the word **solace** mean?

    A. comfort
    B. silence
    C. movement
    D. beauty

3. Which tone is created through the author's word choices?

    A. jolly
    B. forgetful
    C. careless
    D. reflective

4. How does the speaker in "Age" feel about the sea? Use details from the passage to support your answer.

# "THE PLANTING OF THE APPLE TREE"
*by William Cullen Bryant*

Come, let us plant the apple tree.
Cleave the tough greensward with
 the spade;
Wide let its hollow bed be made;
There gently lay the roots, and there
Sift the dark mold with kindly care,
And press it o'er them tenderly,
As round the sleeping infant's feet
We softly fold the cradle sheet;
So plant we the apple tree.

What plant we in this apple tree?
Buds, which the breath of summer
 days
Shall lengthen into leafy sprays;
Boughs where the thrush, with
 crimson breast,
Shall haunt, and sing, and hide her
 nest;
We plant, upon the sunny lea,
A shadow for the noontide hour,
A shelter from the summer shower,
When we plant the apple tree.

What plant we in this apple tree?
Sweets for a hundred flowery
 springs,
To load the May wind's restless
 wings,
When, from the orchard row, he
 pours
Its fragrance through our open
 doors;
A world of blossoms for the bee,
Flowers for the sick girl's silent
 room,
For the glad infant sprigs of bloom,
We plant with the apple tree.

What plant we in this apple tree?
Fruits that shall swell in sunny
 June,
And redden in the August noon,
And drop, when gentle airs come by,
That fan the blue September sky,
While children come, with cries of
 glee,
And seek them where the fragrant
 grass
Betrays their bed to those who pass,
At the foot of the apple tree.

And when, above this apple tree,
The winter stars are quivering
 bright,
The winds go howling through the
 night,
Girls, whose young eyes o'erflow
 with mirth,
Shall peel its fruit by cottage hearth,
And guests in prouder homes shall
 see,
Heaped with the grape of Cintra's
 vine,
And golden orange of the line,
The fruit of the apple tree.

The fruitage of this apple tree,
Winds and our flag of stripe and star
Shall bear to coasts that lie afar,
Where men shall wonder at the
 view,
And ask in what fair groves they
 grew;
And sojourners beyond the sea
Shall think of childhood's careless
 day,
And long, long hours of summer
 play,
In the shade of the apple tree.

Each year shall give this apple tree
A broader flush of roseate bloom,
A deeper maze of verdurous gloom,
And loosen, when the frost-clouds
 lower,
The crisp brown leaves in thicker
 shower.

The years shall come and pass, but we
Shall hear no longer, where we lie,
The summer's songs, the autumn's sigh,
In the boughs of the apple tree.

And time shall waste this apple tree.
Oh, when its aged branches throw
Thin shadows on the ground below,
Shall fraud and force and iron will
Oppress the weak and helpless still?
What shall the tasks of mercy be,
Amid the toils, the strifes, the tears
Of those who live when length of years
Is wasting this apple tree?
"Who planted this old apple tree?
The children of that distant day
Thus to some aged man shall say;
The gray-haired man shall answer them:
"A poet of the land was he,
Born in the rude but good old times;
'Tis said he made some quaint old rhymes
On planting the apple tree."

1. Which statement is best supported by this passage?

    A. Apple trees are not useful trees.
    B. Apples are the most valuable fruit.
    C. Apple trees can live for many years.
    D. Apples are only eaten in America.

2. Which tone is created through the author's word choices?

    A. sadness
    B. anger
    C. humor
    D. love

3. "Cleave the tough greensward with the spade;"

   The author uses this phrase to instruct the listener to

   A. stop to appreciate a tasty apple.
   B. relax under a tree after a difficult day.
   C. use a shovel to dig the hard earth.
   D. cut the apple tree down with an axe.

4. What is the most important task of the apple tree?

   A. to produce fruit
   B. to inspire poems
   C. to give children shade
   D. to make a lovely smell

5. What is the last stanza of this poem mostly about?

   A. what happens when the tree grows old
   B. how to make the tree continue to grow
   C. other types of trees that can be planted
   D. special ways that the apple tree can be used

6. Who planted the apple tree? What makes you think so? Use details from the passage to support your answer.

# AMERICAN INDIAN SETTLEMENT IN OHIO

1. The first humans to enter Ohio came as early as 12,000 to 10,000 B.C.E. They are known as "Paleo-Indians." These people collected into small hunting and foraging groups. They roamed through the area following herds of mastodon and mammoth. Virtually the only remaining archeological evidence of Paleo-Indians are their fluted arrow points and the fossilized bones of their prey.

2. The Archaic Period lasted from 7000 to 800 B.C.E. During this time, tool making of cold-hammered copper became common. Archaic Indians depended upon fishing, hunting, and gathering. Small nomadic groups grew in number and density. Archaic Indians settled only seasonally in campsites in rock shelters near streams, along bluff edges and the flood plain. (Natural processes have destroyed most of these sites.)

3. Toward the end of this era, groups established territories. This allowed for the beginning of long-distance trading systems between groups.

4. The next era, the Early and Middle Woodland Period, occurred from 800 B.C.E. to 500 C.E. The native people during this time relied on maize and squash agriculture, and the growing human population become more sedentary. Villages along the edge of the flood plain continued to expand. They were occupied from the spring through the fall harvest.

5. One Early Woodland Period culture, the Adena culture, emerged about 300 years before the Common Era and lasted until about 200 C.E. in some areas. These prehistoric people cultivated squash, sunflowers, marsh elder, and knotweed. They supplemented their agrarian existence with hunting-and-gathering activities. They typically used pottery, copper, mica, and shells in their everyday work.

6. Most of what is known about the Adena derives from their treatment of their dead. Most deceased were cremated. Some individuals were selected to be encased in log tombs. These were subsequently covered by mounds of dirt. Adjacent burials, and even burials on top of previous mounds, resulted in even larger mounds. Some Adena mounds have been identified at almost ninety feet high, though most are small and contain a single burial.

7. Partially stemming from the Adena people was the Hopewell culture. Many Hopewellian cultural practices show continuity with the Adena. The town of Hopeton was typical of Hopewellian villages. The entire complex featured mounds of varying appearance. The smallest mounds had but one burial and measured about three feet high and twenty-five feet across. The village also had three crematories, places for the burning of the dead.

8. Around 400 C.E., the Hopewell culture began to weaken. We can only speculate as to their situation. Disease, dwindling food supplies, changing climate, and pressure from outside enemies have all been suggested as reasons why the Hopewell culture changed to a pattern known as "Late Woodland" or "Mississippian."

9   From 1000 to 1350 C.E., summer agrarian villages along the edge of the forest revealed an increased density of semi-permanent habitation. Mound building stopped. By the year 1000, a people known as "Fort Ancient" occupied parts of Ohio. They were principally village-based corn growers.

10  However, shortly before European contact, most if not all sites seem to have been abandoned. The latest radiocarbon-dated prehistoric sites date from 1620 C.E. This corresponds with the earliest historic accounts from fur traders. They did not find any American Indian habitation there from 1640 to 1720. One reason was that a series of raids by rival Iroquois tribes who were armed with firearms may have chased away the original people.

11  By the time the first European explorers and settlers came to Ohio in the 17th and 18th centuries, there were many American Indian tribes inhabiting the land. Ottawa from the western Great Lakes soon moved into northeast. They settled in small villages along Lake Erie and south into the Cuyahoga Valley. Wyandot, Mingo, Miami, Shawnee, and Delaware peoples also moved into Ohio.

12  The most enduring American Indian legacy in the Cuyahoga Valley is its name. The most popular translation is "the crooked river," but the "place of the jawbone" and "place of the wing" are also acceptable.

13  After a series of battles in which Americans moved into the Ohio Territory, many native American Indian tribes moved out. The Treaty of Greenville in 1795 took away American Indian claims in most of Ohio. Shortly afterward, most American Indians left the region.


1. Why were the Iroquois most likely able to chase other tribes out of Ohio?

    A. The Iroquois had an older culture.
    B. The Iroquois did not build mounds.
    C. The Iroquois grew more corn.
    D. The Iroquois had better weapons.


2. What did Ohio's native people do during the Archaic Period?

    A. established permanent homes
    B. established stable territories
    C. began long-distance trading
    D. created hammered-copper tools

3. "They **supplemented** their agrarian existence with hunting-and-gathering activities."

   What does the word **supplemented** mean?

   A. learned about
   B. added to
   C. gave back
   D. started again

4. Which American Indian group became known for their fluted arrow points?

   A. Archaic Indians
   B. Paleo-Indians
   C. Early Woodland Indians
   D. Middle Woodland Indians

5. What was the purpose of the Adena mounds?

   A. burial of the dead
   B. defense from enemies
   C. gathering of water
   D. growing of corn

6. What is the purpose of the information in parentheses in paragraph 2?

   A. to divide the topics in the passage in an orderly way
   B. to describe the appearance of ancient sites
   C. to explain why some sites cannot be found today
   D. to explain the difficult words in the passage

7. Why does the author most likely explain Adena burial practices in such detail? Use details from the passage to support your answer.

# EUROPEAN SETTLEMENTS IN OHIO

1. In laying plans for the development of the western lands, the abilities of America's revolutionary leaders were at their best. In the first place, the seven states that had some sort of title to tracts extending westward to the Mississippi wisely yielded these claims to the nation. Thus, a single, national domain was created. This could then be dealt with in accordance with a consistent policy.

2. In the second place, Congress, as early as 1780, pledged the national government to dispose of the western lands for the common benefit. They promised that they should be "settled and formed into distinct republican states, which shall become members of the federal union, and have the same rights of sovereignty, freedom; and independence as the other states."

3. Finally, the Northwest Ordinance of 1787 mapped out a scheme of government adapted to the liberty-loving, yet law-abiding, populations of the frontier. It was based on the broad principles of democracy. It was flexible to permit necessary changes as the scattered settlements developed, first into organized territories and then into states.

4. The Northwest Ordinance was remarkable in that it had been framed for a territory that had practically no white population. In a sense, it did not belong to the United States at all. Back in 1768, Sir William Johnson's Treaty of Fort Stanwix had made the Ohio River the boundary between the white and American Indian races of the West. Nobody at the close of the Revolution supposed that this division would be adhered to. The Northwest had not been won to provide an American Indian reserve.

5. Nonetheless, the arrangements of 1768 were inherited. The nation considered them binding except insofar as they would be modified from time to time by new agreements. The first such agreement affecting the Northwest was concluded in 1785. George Rogers Clark and two other commissioners negotiated with native American Indian tribes. The United States gained title to the southeastern half of the present state of Ohio. The plan was to survey the lands and raise revenue by selling them. Treaties during the next thirty years gradually transferred the whole of the Northwest from American Indian hands to those of the new nation.

6. Officially, the United States recognized the strength of the American Indian claims. The pioneers seeking homes, however, were not so certain to do so. From about the year 1775, the country south of the Ohio filled rapidly with settlers from Virginia and the Carolinas. By 1788, the white population beyond the Blue Ridge was believed to be over 100,000.

7. For a decade, only occasional hunters, traders, and explorers had trod the "American Indian side," as the north shore was called. As time passed, though, the frontiersmen grew bolder. By 1780, they began to plant camps and cabins on the rich bottomlands of the Miami, the Scioto, and the Muskingum. When they heard that the British

claims in the West had been surrendered, they assumed that whatever they could take was theirs. They had little patience with the American Indian claims.

8    In 1785, Colonel Harmar, commanding at Fort Pitt, sent a force down the river to drive the intruders back. His agents returned with the report that the Virginians and Kentuckians were moving into the forbidden country "by the forties and fifties." They seemed intent on staying there. To keep the settlers back, Fort Harmar was built at the mouth of the Muskingum.

9    The close of the Revolution brought greater migration to the West. It also brought more speculation in western land. On March 3, 1786, General Rufus Putnam and some other army officers met at the "Bunch of Grapes" Tavern in Boston. They decided to form an "Ohio Company" to claim land in the region.

10   Dr. Manasseh Cutler—"preacher, lawyer, doctor, statesman, scientist, land speculator"—was sent off to New York to push the matter in Congress. The upshot was that Congress allowed the sale of one and a half million acres east of the Scioto to the Ohio Company. As time went by, the small town they built there thrived.

11   Land speculators are confirmed optimists. Putnam, Cutler, and their associates were correct in believing that the Ohio country was at the start of a period of remarkable development. There was one serious obstacle—the American Indians. Repeated expeditions from Kentucky had pushed most of the tribes northward to the headwaters of the Miami, Scioto, and Wabash. The Treaty of 1785 was supposed to keep them there. However, it was futile to expect such an arrangement to prove lasting unless it was steadily backed up with force.

12   In their villages in the forests of northern Ohio and Indiana, the American Indians grew sullen and angry. As they saw their favorite hunting grounds slipping from their grasp, they felt upset. Those who had taken part in the cession repented their generosity. Those who had no part in it pronounced it unfair and refused to consider themselves bound by it. Swiftly, the idea took hold that the oncoming wave must be rolled back before it was too late. "White man shall not plant corn north of the Ohio!" became the rallying cry.

1.  What is the purpose of the quotation describing Manasseh Cutler in paragraph 10?

    A.  to show his relationship with the American Indians
    B.  to explain the kinds of values he held dear
    C.  to suggest that he was a busy and influential man
    D.  to describe the places where he once lived

2. What is this passage mostly about?

   A. the American push into American Indian territory in Ohio
   B. the American Revolutionary War on the Ohio border
   C. the American Indians who had lived in Ohio for hundreds of years
   D. the American Indians who prepared for war against whites

3. Which treaty made the Ohio River the boundary between the whites and American Indians?

   A. Treaty of Fort Stanwix
   B. Treaty of 1785
   C. Northwest Ordinance
   D. Louisiana Purchase

4. The author most likely wrote this passage in order to

   A. gather aid for American Indians in Ohio
   B. describe ways people can find new homes
   C. persuade readers to move into the West
   D. explain how whites first moved to Ohio

5. How did Colonel Harmar attempt to drive back intruders?

   A. He hired surveyors.
   B. He sent soldiers.
   C. He sold land shares.
   D. He signed a treaty.

6. Why did seven states give up their titles to western lands?

   A. to avoid attacks by American Indians
   B. to let the national government deal with them
   C. to move west and fight for the land
   D. to create a reservation for American Indians

7. "Land speculators are confirmed optimists."

   What does the author mean when she describes speculators as **confirmed optimists**?

   A. They always look on the bright side.
   B. They always ask for permission.
   C. They need to be told everything twice.
   D. They only believe what they see.

8. Do you think that any arrangement could have satisfied the American Indians, the land speculators, and the land buyers? Why or why not? Use details from the passage to support your answer.

# CLIMATE AND WEATHER

**Background**

1   "Climate" refers to the average conditions of a place. "Weather" refers to the current conditions. Weather is the state of the air with respect to heat or cold, wetness or dryness, calm or storm, clearness or cloudiness.

**Ohio's Climate**

2   The climate of an area is determined by latitude, elevation, prevailing air currents, and proximity to oceans and lakes. Ohio is located between 38 and 42 degrees north latitude. It is at low elevations. It is in the eastern interior of North America, and is south of Lake Erie. These factors have created the climate in Ohio.

3   Here are some fun facts about Ohio's climate:

- Ohioans experience four distinct seasons, large seasonal temperature ranges, and frequent precipitation.
- Counties near Lake Erie record heavier snowfall than other parts of the state. They average fifteen inches more than in southern Ohio.
- Nearness to Lake Erie also prevents spring frosts. That extends the growing season. The hills of southeastern Ohio affect the weather in that region.
- Average temperatures for January in Ohio are less than 32° Fahrenheit.
- In July, average temperatures exceed 75° Fahrenheit.
- The lowest temperature recorded in the state prior to 1903 was -39° Fahrenheit (recorded at Milligan, Perry County, on February 10, 1899).
- The highest temperature recorded in the state was 113° Fahrenheit (recorded at Gallipolis on July 21, 1934).
- Precipitation averages between 30 and 40 inches per year in Ohio.
- In 1990, there was a record-breaking 51.33 inches of precipitation.
- By contrast, 1930 was the driest year, with only 26.59 inches average precipitation.

**Extreme Weather Conditions**

*Droughts*

4   Droughts, or severe and persistent dry spells, occur about once a decade in Ohio. They often cause significant problems for Ohio farmers.

*Floods*

5   The opposite problem—flooding—results from either intense local rainstorms or prolonged periods of heavy rain across a wide area. This extreme weather condition is most frequent in winter and spring.

6   Floods soak normally dry areas and usually occur around bodies of water. Ohio has more than three thousand named rivers and streams, including the Cuyahoga, Great Miami, Little Miami, Maumee, Ohio, Olentangy, Sandusky, and Scioto. Some of these waters, like the Ohio and the Miamis, are particularly likely to flood.

7   Toledo experienced particularly damaging floods of the Maumee River in 1867 and 1881. In 1883, the Cuyahoga River flooded. Also in 1883, the Ohio River rose to a record height of 66.3 feet in Cincinnati. (Its ordinary height is 50 feet.) The following year was even worse. The river set a new record of 71.1 feet in Cincinnati. It washed out bridges at Zanesville and McConnelsville. It submerged Gallipolis, Ironton, Portsmouth, and Ripley.

8   In March 1913, massive flooding again devastated the state. Columbus, Dayton, Hamilton, and Tiffin sustained some of the worst damage. Throughout the state, nearly five hundred people lost their lives. The cost of the flood was estimated to be $100 million. Because of the events of 1913, the Miami Conservancy District was established to prevent future flooding by constructing dams and levees. Flood-control efforts were also established in other parts of the state.

9   These efforts were tested in January, 1937, a terrible month for flooding. Along the Ohio River, from Gallipolis to the Ohio-Indiana border, new high-water marks were set in every town. Portsmouth and Cincinnati were particularly affected. In the Queen City, waters rose to nearly eighty feet, a new record. Dayton and the Miami Valley were spared, however. Flood-control efforts in the region protected it from harm.

*Snowstorms*

10  Six or more inches of snowfall in one day constitute a heavy snow in Ohio. In northern Ohio, particularly along the shore of Lake Erie, heavy snows are expected several times a year. They occur less frequently in other parts of the state.

11  Marietta experienced the most extreme storm of the early settlement period in February 1818. Twenty-six inches of snow fell. In Cincinnati in January 1863, 20 inches accumulated in twenty-four hours. That record still stands. Twenty-two inches of snow blanketed Cleveland in January 1878. The same amount fell on Toledo in February 1900. In April 1901, Gratiot (near Zanesville) got forty-two inches of snow in fifty-six hours. The whole state was affected by the blizzard of 1918. Temperatures dropped rapidly into negative numbers. High gusting winds blew heavy snowfall into drifts.

12  In January 1978, an even more severe blizzard struck the state. Average winds were 45–60 miles per hour with gusts exceeding one hundred miles per hour. Wind chill temperatures were up to –60° Fahrenheit. Heavy snow fell. Power, water, telephones, and transportation routes were disrupted for up to five days. Snowdrifts were high enough to cover houses and collapse roofs. The Red Cross, Ohio National Guard, Army Corps of Engineers, and federal troops were called in to help with relief efforts.

1. The author most likely wrote this passage in order to

   A. persuade readers to visit Ohio's towns.
   B. describe great Ohio places for tourists.
   C. entertain the reader with a lively tale.
   D. list facts and figures about certain conditions.


2. What is the purpose of the bulleted list in the passage?

   A. to divide the topics into broad categories
   B. to present varied pieces of information
   C. to show the importance of climate in Ohio
   D. to give opinions from a resident of Ohio


3. Which area of Ohio gets more snow but fewer spring frosts?

   A. Lake Erie
   B. dams and levees
   C. Ohio-Indiana border
   D. hilly regions


4. What was the most likely reason for including the information about droughts in this passage?

   A. to show that snow does not melt quickly in Ohio
   B. to show that droughts are more dangerous than floods
   C. to show that there are more droughts than snowstorms
   D. to show that having too little precipitation is harmful


5. Which river flooded four Ohio towns in 1884?

   A. Ohio River
   B. Cuyahoga River
   C. Maumee River
   D. Miami River

6. "Six or more inches of snowfall in one day **constitute** a heavy snow in Ohio."

   What does the word **constitute** mean?

   A. damage
   B. fall down
   C. make up
   D. danger

7. "Along the Ohio River, from Gallipolis to the Ohio-Indiana border, **new high-water marks were set** in every town."

   What does the author mean when he says that **new high-water marks were set**?

   A. New protections were built.
   B. Many people lost their lives.
   C. New rivers and streams formed.
   D. The water rose higher than ever.

8. Why does Ohio's climate vary from region to region? Use specific examples to support your ideas.

# THE WESTERN RESERVE AND THE CUYAHOGA VALLEY

1. The first Euro-American settlement in the Cuyahoga Valley began in 1786. Moravian missionary John Heckewelder built a mission he called "Pilgerruh" along the river. He abandoned it the following year.

2. Two French traders also established posts. One was at French House in the general vicinity of the junction of Tinkers Creek and the Cuyahoga River. The other was at Portage Path. (A popular legend holds that craftsmen at a Portage military post manufactured three gunboats. They were part of Oliver Hazard Perry's Lake Erie fleet and played key roles in the September 10, 1813, American victory.)

3. Despite these small habitations, the valley remained a "quiet backwater" for several decades. However, it soon became the center of a conflict.

4. In the late 1700s, four states claimed the land west of Pennsylvania. This was due largely to confusion caused by overlapping land grants from the British crown. New York, Virginia, Massachusetts, and Connecticut all claimed lands in the "Northwest Territory." The resulting disputes became heated and sometimes violent.

5. To end the turmoil, the states, beginning with New York in 1780, relinquished their claims to the national government. The last to cede its claim was Connecticut in 1786. However, Connecticut officials reserved a strip of territory along the south shore of Lake Erie. It stretched one hundred and twenty miles west from Pennsylvania with a southern boundary at the 41st parallel. Congress officially recognized the area as "The Western Reserve of Connecticut." The Cuyahoga River lay entirely within this Western Reserve.

6. In 1795, Connecticut established a commission to administer the sale of the three-million-acre Western Reserve. Officials also set aside land along Lake Erie for Connecticut citizens who had lost property from British bombardments of the coast during the Revolutionary War. The area was henceforth called the "Firelands." It is known today as Erie and Huron Counties. On September 1, 1795, the commission sold the land, at forty cents an acre, for $1.2 million. That amount was placed in a special fund to benefit schools.

7. The state issued quit-claim deeds to the purchasers, a syndicate of 35 men. They had formed the Connecticut Land Company. Beginning in April 1796, the company surveyed land east of the Cuyahoga River into townships. At the mouth of the Cuyahoga River, the city of "Cleveland" was plotted. It was named after the Connecticut Land Company's general agent, General Moses Cleaveland. On July 4, 1805, American Indians ceded lands west of the Cuyahoga River. The remaining Western Reserve survey work soon began.

8   Settlement of the Western Reserve came only incrementally as Connecticut Land Company proprietors sold off their individual holdings. Settlers came principally from New England through Buffalo, New York, and then by way of Lake Erie. Some hauled their boats up the Cuyahoga River into the valley and beyond. Others herded their cattle over the cleared-off, surveyed range lines. Other settlers used the American Indians' "Mahoning Trail." Settlement increased following the War of 1812. Many of Commodore Perry's men purchased land in the area. Deadly New England frosts brought an influx of Connecticut farmers to the Western Reserve in the summer of 1816.

9   The Cuyahoga Valley was also slow to be settled largely because of its geographical isolation. Farmers found the valley heavily forested. Valley walls, in addition to being steep and rugged, tended to also be unstable. Subsistence farmers there led hard lives. Other places had fewer topographical obstacles, better communication systems, and more commercial development opportunities.

10  As the population around Cleveland began to expand, Cuyahoga County formed in 1807. It encompassed the northern half of the Cuyahoga Valley. The southern half of the valley was incorporated into Summit County when it formed in 1840.


1.  This passage is most similar to

    A.  a brochure on tourist attractions
    B.  an article on local history
    C.  a list of figures from an almanac
    D.  an entry in a dictionary


2.  Where did John Heckewelder build a mission?

    A.  Portage Path
    B.  French House
    C.  Pilgerruh
    D.  Tinkers Creek

3. Why was farming difficult in the Cuyahoga Valley?

   A. People were not allowed to settle there.
   B. States would not allow farming in the area.
   C. The land was far too expensive to purchase.
   D. The land was covered with heavy forests.

4. The author most likely wrote this passage in order to

   A. report on early settlement in an area
   B. entertain readers with an exciting story
   C. convince readers to move to an area
   D. give directions to begin a mission

5. Congress recognized the Western Reserve as belonging to

   A. Massachusetts
   B. American Indians
   C. New York
   D. Connecticut

6. The money from the sale of the Western Reserve was used to fund

   A. schools
   B. American Indians
   C. farmers
   D. American soldiers

7. "Settlement of the Western Reserve came only **incrementally** as Connecticut Land Company proprietors sold off their individual holdings."

   What does the word **incrementally** mean?

   A. piece by piece
   B. large and small
   C. east and west
   D. best to worst

8. What most likely attracted settlers to the Cuyahoga Valley? Use details from the passage to support your answer.

# OHIO WARS

## Introduction

1  Between 1650 and 1700, the American Indian tribes of the Iroquois Confederacy claimed what is now Ohio. The Iroquois wanted the territory to hunt beaver, which they would then trade to the French. In what became known as the "Beaver Wars," the Iroquois forced tribes native to the region to join the Iroquois Confederacy, move westward, or be destroyed.

2  Early in the eighteenth century, France and Britain had begun a contest for control of the Ohio Country. This contest was not settled until the victory of the British in the French and Indian War in 1763. Conflicts between American Indians and Europeans continued throughout the coming years as alliances shifted and waves of settlers hungered for more land.

## American Revolution (1776–1783)

3  The American Revolution set the United States at war with Great Britain. In the Ohio Country, American Indians, and American military forces met in a series of skirmishes. Many of the American Indian groups, including the Delaware, Wyandot, Miami, and Ottawa tribes, joined with the British. They hoped to prevent American settlements in the Ohio Country.

4  American troops at Fort Laurens (Tuscarawas County) withstood two joint British and American Indian sieges in 1779. Finally, the fort was abandoned. The next year, in the Battle of Piqua, George Rogers Clark led a raid on Shawnee villages near present-day Springfield, Ohio. Later still, a force led by Colonel David Williamson attacked a group of Christian American Indians who had been accused of crimes against white settlers.

5  Colonel William Crawford defeated a British and American Indian force in the Battle of the Olentangy. Crawford's forces were divided, however. He and some of his men were taken prisoner by a group of Delaware American Indians. Crawford was cruelly punished as revenge for the Gnadenhutten attack.

6  The Peace of Paris (1783) formally ended the American Revolution. Under its terms, Britain recognized its former colony's independence. Britain kept control of Canada and gave Florida to Spain, which had been America's ally in the Revolution.

## American Indian Wars (1790–1794)

7  As settlers flocked to the Northwest Territory after the Revolution, the British continued to support American Indian tribes in the area. General Josiah Harmar attempted to calm the American Indian groups led by Blue Jacket and Little Turtle in 1790. He was defeated near present-day Fort Wayne, Indiana.

8   President George Washington then ordered General Arthur St. Clair, governor of the Northwest Territory, to defeat the American Indians and force them from southern Ohio. However, the American Indians, led by Miami Chief Little Turtle, surprised St. Clair. They defeated his army while losing only 21 braves. Although St. Clair was later cleared of any misconduct, President Washington ordered St. Clair back to Cincinnati.

9   Washington next sent General "Mad" Anthony Wayne to Ohio to defeat the American Indians. Wayne built a series of forts, including Fort Recovery on the site of St. Clair's defeat, on his march northward. On August 20, 1794, Wayne's army defeated an army of Wyandot, Miami, Ottawa, Delaware, Mingo, Shawnee, and other American Indians at the Battle of Fallen Timbers. Wayne then followed the scattered troops to the British Fort Miami.

10  The British troops refused to help their American Indian allies. On August 3, 1795, the Wyandot, Delaware, Shawnee, Ottawa, Miami, Chippewa, Potawatomi, Wea, Kickapoo, Eel River, Piankashaw, and Kaskaskia tribes signed the Treaty of Greenville. It limited their lands to northwestern Ohio. In return, they received a payment of $20,000 in goods, plus an additional $9,500 in goods per year.

**War of 1812 (1812–1815)**

11  Conflict between the United States and Great Britain did not end with the Revolutionary War. As tensions rose between Britain and the United States, American Indians in Ohio began a recovery. One chief, Tecumseh, and his brother, the Prophet, vowed to restore American Indian lands. General William Henry Harrison led an attack on Prophet's Town in 1811 in the Battle of Tippecanoe. Although they were victorious, Harrison's army suffered heavy losses. (He later successfully campaigned for political office with the slogan, "Tippecanoe and Tyler, too!")

12  In June 1812, the United States declared war on Great Britain in protest of British attacks on American ships and impressment of U.S. seamen into the British navy. The war was fought on land and sea in Canada, the Northwest Territory, and the southern states. Much of Washington, D.C., was burned.

13  General Harrison was appointed commander-in-chief of the Northwestern Army. He built Fort Meigs, named after Ohio governor Return J. Meigs, near present-day Perrysburg. Supplying the fort was difficult. Artillery and food had to be carried through the Black Swamp. Nonetheless, Fort Meigs withstood several assaults by British troops. An attack on Fort Stephenson near Fremont forced Major George Croghan to defend the fort with only one cannon, nicknamed "Old Betsy."

14  In one of the most significant battles of the war, Colonel Oliver Hazard Perry defeated the British at the Battle of Lake Erie in September 1813. The British Captain Robert Barclay surrendered his entire fleet. Harrison learned that Perry had effectively cut the British supply line through Perry's message: "We have met the enemy and they are ours."

15  The Treaty of Ghent established peace in 1814, although fighting continued into 1815.

1. What was most remarkable about the defense of Fort Stephenson?

   A. It was accomplished with only one cannon.
   B. Local American Indian tribes helped with it.
   C. It cut the British supply line in the region.
   D. It directed the war toward the southern states.


2. What is the purpose of the words in parentheses in the section titled "War of 1812"?

   A. to give examples of the way people spoke long ago
   B. to show why Harrison was a better soldier than a president
   C. to show how events could influence future happenings
   D. to explain the reasons why many presidents use slogans


3. The Ohio Indians lost most of Ohio when they agreed to the terms of the

   A. Peace of Paris.
   B. Treaty of Greenville.
   C. Treaty of Ghent.
   D. Northwest Ordinance.


4. "In the Ohio Country, American Indians, and American military forces met in a series of **skirmishes**."

   What does the word **skirmishes** mean?

   A. lengthy treaties
   B. difficult languages
   C. unusual settlements
   D. brief battles

5. Where did William Henry Harrison have the greatest military success?

   A. Gnadenhutten
   B. Fort Meigs
   C. Tippecanoe
   D. Lake Erie

6. What does this passage suggest about the Iroquois Confederacy?

   A. They were enemies of France.
   B. They were allies of Britain.
   C. They were defeated in the war.
   D. They were powerful warriors.

7. The author most likely included the information in the first two paragraphs of the passage to

   A. explain the history of the region before the American Revolution.
   B. persuade readers to sympathize with the Ohio American Indians.
   C. describe the French and Indian War in great detail.
   D. explain each treaty between native American Indian people and settlers.

8. "Although St. Clair was later **cleared of any misconduct**, President Washington ordered St. Clair back to Cincinnati."

   What does the author mean when she says that St. Clair was **cleared of any misconduct**?

   A. He was given a lower rank.
   B. He was declared not guilty.
   C. He was unknown to others.
   D. He was committing crimes.

9. Which battle mentioned in the passage was probably the most important? Use information from the passage to support your answer.

# OHIO STATE SYMBOLS

### The State Animal

1   The Ohio government adopted the white-tailed deer as the state animal in May 1988. The state's largest game animal is found in all of Ohio's eighty-eight counties, even though about eighty percent of the herd lives in hilly eastern Ohio.

### The State Insect

2   In June 1975, Ohio declared the common ladybug, officially named the "Ladybird Beetle," the state insect. Its attractive markings and helpful eating habits made the ladybug a worthy representative of the state.

### The State Bird

3   Ohio's official bird is the cardinal. A permanent resident of Ohio, the cardinal is known for its clear, strong song and brilliant plumage.

### The State Fossil

4   Ohio's state fossil is the isotelus, more commonly known as the trilobite. This now-extinct sea animal called Ohio home when salt water covered the state millions of years ago. Resembling the modern horseshoe crab, the trilobite is about fourteen inches long.

### The State Flag

5   Adopted in 1902, the state flag features a large blue triangle which represents Ohio's hills and valleys. The flags stripes represent roads and waterways. The white circle with its red center stands for the "O" in Ohio. It also suggests Ohio's famous nickname, "The Buckeye State."

### The State Seal

6   The current design of the Great Seal of the state of Ohio was officially adopted in 1967. A sheath of wheat represents Ohio's agricultural strength. Seventeen arrows on the left and the seventeen rays around the sun symbolize Ohio's position as the seventeenth state admitted to the Union. The background contains a picture of Mount Logan, with the sun rising behind it. The Scioto River flows between the mountain and a large field.

### The State Motto

7   In 1959, the Ohio adopted the state's motto, "With God all things are possible." An earlier motto, "Imperium in Imperio" (An Empire within an Empire), was adopted in 1865. It was revoked two years later because citizens thought it sounded conceited.

**The State Flower**

8   The red carnation was adopted as Ohio's state flower in 1904 in memory of President William McKinley. The Ohio native always wore a red carnation in his lapel.

**The State Tree**

9   The nickname for Ohio and its inhabitants—Buckeye—became official in 1953. The state government named the American horse chestnut (or the Ohio buckeye) the state tree. The buckeye tree gets its name from its large, brown seeds, which resemble the eyes of the eastern white-tailed deer.

**The State Gemstone**

10  Flint has been the state gemstone since 1965. The American Indians used this smooth, hard rock to make knives, spear points, and arrowheads. Later, Ohio settlers used it other various purposes.

**The State Reptile**

11  The black racer snake was named Ohio's official reptile in 1995. Jacob Mercer, a fourth-grade student, sent a letter to state representatives and senators suggesting that Ohio name an official reptile. He and his classmates decided on the black racer snake because it's found in all eighty-eight counties. Known as the "farmer's friend," the snake is a helpful animal that feeds on disease-carrying rodents.

**The State Song**

12  In 1969, "Beautiful Ohio" became the state song. Mary Earl composed the music and Ballard McDonald wrote the original words. In 1989, new words were added by Youngstown lawyer Wilbert McBride.

**The State Rock Song**

13  "Hang On Sloopy" became the state rock song in 1985. Celina-born guitarist Rick Derringer composed the music and rock band the McCoys recorded the song in 1965.


1.  What is this passage mostly about?

    A.  how Ohio became part of the Union
    B.  why every state needs its own song
    C.  the different state symbols of Ohio
    D.  where to find your state's symbols

2. What is the purpose of the bold headings throughout the passage?

   A. to capture the readers' attention
   B. to make the passage easy to read
   C. to highlight the important sections
   D. to tell the author's point of view

3. What do the stripes symbolize on Ohio's state flag?

   A. roads and waterways
   B. the state's people
   C. hills and valleys
   D. the state's nickname

4. What does the number seventeen represent on the state seal?

   A. the 17 counties found in Ohio
   B. Ohio's position as the 17th state in the union
   C. the fact that the 17th president was from Ohio
   D. the original 17 settlers of Ohio

5. "It was **revoked** two years later because citizens thought it sounded conceited."

   What does the word **revoked** mean?

   A. related
   B. casually referred
   C. requested
   D. made void

6. Who suggested that the black racer snake be named Ohio's state reptile?
   A. Wilbert McBride
   B. Jacob Mercer
   C. William McKinley
   D. Ballard McDonald

7. Why do you think that states have state symbols? Use information from the passage to support your answer.

# MIGRATION TO OHIO, 1785–1850

1   In 1800, Ohio's population was only forty-five thousand, but just fifty years later it had exceeded two million.

2   Ohio occupied a special position with respect to the early settlement of the Old Northwest. On its southern boundary was the Ohio River, which became a major passageway for migrants moving south and west. After the opening of the Erie Canal in 1825, the northern Great Lakes became a very important westward passage.

3   American-born settlers came to Ohio from three different regions of the United States: New England, the Mid-Atlantic, and the Upland South. Migrants from New England settled primarily in the Connecticut Western Reserve, located in the northeastern part of the state. They also settled in Marietta, Ohio's first authorized settlement. Other New Englanders made their homes in cities like Putnam, Granville, and Worthington.

4   During this period, the largest number of migrants came from the Mid-Atlantic states like Pennsylvania. These people made up forty-three percent of all migrants during the first half of the nineteenth century. Most of the migration traveled along routes through the middle of Ohio. One important route was along Zane's Trace.

5   Migrants from Pennsylvania were mainly Germans and Scots-Irish. Because of this, the middle regions of Ohio have a strong German influence. This is seen in distinctive log-cabin-style homes and barn construction. New Jersey and its neighboring states were also well represented in the settlement of Ohio, largely due to the Symmes Purchase. This was a real estate venture organized by a prominent New Jersey judge, John Cleves Symmes.

6   The majority of southern migrants came to Ohio from Virginia. They settled in the Virginia Military District lands, located in the west-central portion of the state. Southern influence in this region can be seen in the greater number of large farms, the majority of the I-house style of dwelling (long brick houses with a double porch), and the large percentage of residents of Scots-Irish heritage.

7   Overseas immigration contributed to the settlement of Ohio in the early half of the nineteenth century. Many overseas immigrants came to Ohio from the countries of northwest Europe, particularly Germany and Ireland. By 1850, nearly half of Ohio's immigrant population came from various parts of Germany.

8   Irish immigrants also came to Ohio in large numbers. Many came to Ohio seeking economic opportunities that they could no longer find in Ireland due to a large shortage of food. Many Irish immigrants made their homes in Ohio's cities. Employment opportunities in the railroad and canal industries directed Irish immigrants into rural areas as well.

9    Ohio also attracted peoples from many other countries. The English settled in the Western Reserve, while the French overcame a failed settlement in Gallipolis and later put down roots in southeastern Ohio. The Swiss settled in the Pennsylvania Dutch areas, as well as in Monroe and Tuscarawas Counties. The Canadians originally settled in the Refugee Tract of central Ohio, but later migrated to other areas of the state where English-speaking communities already existed.

1. Which Ohio passageway could a settler have used to travel west?

    A. the Sandusky River
    B. Symmes Purchase
    C. the Great Lakes
    D. Zane's Trace

2. The first authorized settlement in Ohio was

    A. Worthington
    B. Marietta
    C. Putnam
    D. Granville

3. Which of the following demonstrates the strong German influence in the middle regions of Ohio?

    A. the large number of farms
    B. the I-house style dwellings
    C. the log-cabin-style houses
    D. the number of large cities

4. The people who settled in the Symmes Purchase were mostly

    A. migrating from New Jersey
    B. looking for job opportunities
    C. of Scots-Irish descent
    D. hoping to start farms

5. Which state sent the most settlers to Ohio?

    A. Connecticut
    B. Pennsylvania
    C. Virginia
    D. New Jersey

6. Who is most likely the intended audience for this passage?

    A. people planning to move to Ohio
    B. people who have friends in Ohio
    C. people researching Ohio's rivers
    D. people interested in Ohio's history

7. Which statement is support by the passage?

    A. There weren't enough jobs for all the people migrating.
    B. Ohio became overcrowded during the late 1800s.
    C. Ohio has been influenced by many groups of people.
    D. There wasn't enough food for all the people migrating.

8. The "Migration to Ohio, 1785–1850" passage is most similar to

    A. a journal entry
    B. a news article
    C. a historical report
    D. a local folk tale

# CANAL AND RAILROAD

1   American leaders knew that the key to developing the continent's vast interior was establishing a good transportation system. The only convenient form of transportation in those days was by water. The easiest way into the interior would be to link the Great Lakes with the nation's river systems. This meant that a series of canals would be needed. As early as 1784, George Washington had come up with a plan to boost the fur trade and interior communications by utilizing the Great Lakes. In 1788, Washington formally proposed canals linking the Cuyahoga, Big Beaver, and Muskingum Rivers. This would allow easy access from the Great Lakes to the Ohio River.

2   Canal-building in the United States reached a feverish pace following the opening of New York's 363-mile Erie Canal. Ohio was especially intrigued by New York's example. High freight charges made it difficult for Ohio's struggling farmers to ship their crops to eastern markets. In 1822, a commission was set up to locate potential canal routes. The Ohio legislature soon authorized the construction of two canals. The Ohio and Erie Canal would run from Cleveland to Portsmouth, and the Miami Canal would run from Cincinnati to Dayton.

3   From Cleveland, the Ohio and Erie Canal route proceeded south along the Cuyahoga River. It then climbed over the Portage Summit at the future site of Akron. From there it was to run to the Tuscarawas, west to the Licking, then to the Scioto at Columbus. Finally, it would make its way south to the Ohio River town of Portsmouth. The canal route was a total of three hundred eight miles, crossing thirteen counties through northeastern, central, and south-central Ohio.

4   The Ohio and Erie Canal's first link opened on July 3, 1827. A group led by Ohio governor Allen Trimble left Portage Summit aboard the *State of Ohio*. The boat wound her way through the Cuyahoga Valley's forty-four locks and three aqueducts. The canal trench itself was forty feet wide at the top and twenty-six feet across at the bottom. The entire canal was completed in 1832.

5   The engineering miracle proved to be an economic wonder as well. Barges could now cross the state in eighty to ninety hours. The Ohio and Erie Canal not only tied Ohio to the rest of the nation, but it also helped to open the interior to other markets in the south and east. Living standards improved with the new prosperity and settlers poured into central Ohio as towns cropped up along the canal.

6   Rivers and canals remained the primary means of transportation in the United States until the coming of railroads. Trains were a quicker, more efficient mode of transportation. They began to eat away at canal revenues in the 1850s. Soon, many canals were controlled by private companies. No longer economically competitive, many canals were abandoned in the 1880s.

7   In the Cuyahoga Valley, the Ohio and Erie Canal was the primary mode of north-south transportation for a half-century. Topographical difficulties temporarily

prevented the construction of a railroad route through the valley to connect Cleveland and Akron. A desire to haul iron ore more cheaply from Canton for the blast furnaces of Cleveland prompted construction of a rail route. Called the "Valley Railroad," the route paralleled the west bank of the Cuyahoga River and the Ohio and Erie Canal. Railroad stations were built at Independence, Boston, and Peninsula. With this vibrant transportation system in place, the subsistence lifestyle disappeared. Farmers stripped most of the valley of its heavy forest cover to till the rich soil for a profit.

8   The Valley Railroad competed with the canal for commerce. Nagging financial problems resulted in the railroad's bankruptcy in 1894. In 1890, it was incorporated into the Baltimore and Ohio Railroad (B&O) system. In 1895, it resumed operations under the name Cleveland Terminal and Valley Railroad. A devastating flood in 1913 ended the operation of the canal in the valley. The B&O maintained passenger service on the Valley Railroad until mid-century.

9   By the turn of the century, a complex road system criss-crossed the valley. Both of the nineteenth-century transportation systems of the Cuyahoga Valley were about to be surpassed by something new—the private automobile.

10  Cleveland's population grew quickly thanks to the Ohio and Erie Canal. A ready food supply was available from the fertile Cuyahoga Valley to the south. New industries sprouted along these water routes. Urban industrial expansion skyrocketed. The town's status as a trade center surged again when rail service arrived in 1852. When high-grade iron ore from the Great Lakes region was mixed with soft Ohio coal to make steel, Cleveland's future as one of America's industrial centers was assured.

11  Akron traces its birth to the canal. The construction of the Pennsylvania and Ohio Canal, linking Akron with Pittsburgh encouraged new expansion. Industries ranging from iron ore smelters to pottery kilns moved to Akron. Grain mills, such as Ferdinand Schumacher's, came as well. This particular mill evolved into the Quaker Oats Company. In 1880, Akron's Benjamin F. Goodrich opened a rubber factory to manufacture carriage and bicycle tires. Similar companies—such as Miller, Seiberling, and Firestone—were also located in Akron. With the advent of the automobile, the rubber-tire industry boomed.

12  As Cleveland and Akron prospered, both cities expanded in the direction of the Cuyahoga Valley. Despite the developing transportation systems, it had remained a quiet backwater. Valley resources were extensively exploited to construct both the canal and railroad routes. Trees not felled for these projects were logged off to clear the land for farming or for homebuilding in the valley or nearby cities. Sandstone was quarried at several sites for the canal's infrastructure. These construction activities in the valley also brought an influx of workers. Once completed, the canal continued to provide employment opportunities. One young man who worked for a short time as a "hoggie," or mule-driver, on the canal was James A. Garfield, a future president of the United States.

1. George Washington felt that interconnected waterways would help

    A. poor farmers
    B. the fur trade
    C. the iron industry
    D. Ohio settlers


2. People in Ohio were inspired by a canal that had been built in

    A. Pittsburgh
    B. Miami
    C. Boston
    D. New York


3. Which statement best describes the author's viewpoint of the Ohio and Erie Canal?

    A. It helped to improve life in central Ohio.
    B. It forced farmers to pay high shipping charges.
    C. It forced many railroads out of business.
    D. It helped many towns to remain quiet and peaceful.


4. What temporarily prevented a railroad route connecting Cleveland and Akron?

    A. competition with canal routes
    B. interference by the government
    C. geographical problems
    D. financial difficulties


5. A railroad was finally built in Cuyahoga Valley because of

    A. the demand for iron ore
    B. the failure of the canal
    C. farmers' need to ship crops
    D. Ohioans' desire to travel


6. Which of the following ended the operation of the canal in Cuyahoga Valley?

    A. new railroad routes
    B. a powerful flood
    C. private companies
    D. new technology

7. "With the **advent** of the automobile, the rubber-tire industry boomed."

   What does the word **advent** mean?
   A. failure
   B. transformation
   C. coming
   D. sample

8. Which do you think was most important to Cleveland's growth—canals, railroads, or automobiles? Why? Use information from the passage to support your answer.

# OHIO WOMEN

**Home and Work**

1   In early Ohio, much of a woman's day consisted of the exhausting and time-consuming tasks of cleaning, cooking, doing laundry, and making clothing. Each of these was a far more drawn-out process than it is today.

2   Between 1820 and the Civil War, the growth of new industries helped to create a new middle class in America. Families in the middle and upper classes hired servants and purchased commercially-produced clothing and food. These changes relieved some of the drudgery of pioneer life.

3   By the 1850s, women's place in society began to change. The Industrial Revolution created the need for unskilled labor. Women found new opportunities to earn their living in factory jobs. Some women became pioneers in male-dominated professions.

4   The Industrial Revolution also resulted in numerous labor-saving devices, such as sewing machines, washing machines, and carpet sweepers. These allowed wealthier women to have more leisure time. Although women enjoyed some new measure of independence, their legal position remained inferior to men's. It was illegal for married women to own property and they had no legal standing to make decisions concerning their children's welfare.

5   World War I created a labor shortage. This encouraged women to go to work. After the war, and particularly during the Great Depression in the 1930s, women were forced out of the job market. Most of the Depression-era relief programs excluded women as well. In 1941, the entry of the United States into a second world war gave women the chance to work again. Though they received lower wages than the men they had replaced, war work was more lucrative than traditional female occupations. Women's branches of the armed forces were also established, allowing women to serve in the military in times of war. In 1948, women gained the right to serve during peacetime. Civilian women were urged to support the war effort by volunteering for organizations such as the Red Cross and the United Service Organization (USO).

**Women's Clubs**

6   Clubs served an important role in women's lives, particularly those women of the upper middle class. Many of the first clubs were Bible societies. Women were encouraged to expand their church activities by attending weekly meetings for Bible readings. The women's club movement began to change during the 1860s when clubs shifted their focus from religion to literature.

7   Women's clubs reflected the cultural ideals of the times and the goals of moral and domestic perfection. The clubs also provided forums for efforts to uphold or alter gender roles. In a society that encouraged women to stay at home, club membership represented an acceptable activity, unlike campaigning for the right to vote. Many clubwomen actually opposed the suffrage movement. In the 1870–1890s, women's

clubs expanded into art, drama, music, and other cultural studies. Some turned their attention to community issues such as medicine and education reform. Though these clubs did not specifically focus on women's rights, they did extend the women's sphere outside of the home.

**Reform Movements**

8   The first political involvement many women had was through the abolitionist movement. Some women noticed the parallels between themselves and slaves, since neither women nor African Americans were permitted to vote or control property and both encountered limited educational and occupational opportunities.

9   Many of the women who participated in abolitionist endeavors joined the women's rights movement. The movement's three main goals included securing economic progress, legal equality, and, most importantly, women's right to vote. The first women's rights convention in the United States was held in Seneca Falls, New York, in 1848. The second was held in Salem, Ohio, in April 1850, and was largely comprised of antislavery radicals. Betsy Mix Cowles presided over the convention. Its immediate purpose was to petition the Ohio Constitutional Convention for equal rights. Another convention was called in Akron, Ohio, in 1851 to encourage lawmakers to legally extend the rights provided to women under Ohio's constitution. This convention was the scene of Sojourner Truth's eloquent "Ain't I a Woman?" speech. Annual conventions were held for several years afterwards. It was not until 1861 that married women were given the right to own real estate and to maintain personal property.

10  Women in Ohio had to wait until 1920, when Ohio ratified the 19th Amendment, which guaranteed all American women the right to vote. Suffrage supporters in Ohio rejoiced once voting rights had become universal for all citizens.

11  The 1960s sparked a new women's movement, concerned with political, educational, and social equality. Title VII of the Civil Rights Act of 1964 barred employers from discriminating by sex, race, color, or ethnicity. The Equal Employment Opportunity Commission was created to enforce the legislation. This measure fell short of the ultimate goal of complete equality between men and women.

12  The National Organization for Women, established in 1966, was one group committed to improving the status of women in the areas of education, employment, and reproductive freedom, among other issues. Toledo native Gloria Steinem founded *Ms.* magazine in 1971 and worked to bring attention to women's issues.

13  Another effort to secure legislative guarantees of women's rights was the Equal Rights Amendment. Although passed by the Senate in 1972, the ERA was ratified by only thirty-five states, three fewer than were needed to enact the amendment.

14  Despite that failure, a landmark event did occur in 1972: the passage of the Higher Education Act. This act prohibited discrimination based on sex in educational institutions that receive federal funds. One of the most visible results of Title IX has

been the rise in athletic programs and scholarships for women. Before 1972, all athletic scholarships went to men, but by 2003, thirty percent of scholarship funds were awarded to women.

1. Which of the following helped to create a new middle class in America?

    A. the Great Depression
    B. women's clubs
    C. World War I
    D. new industries

2. "These changes relieved some of the **drudgery** of pioneer life."

    What does the word **drudgery** mean?

    A. regret
    B. labor
    C. boredom
    D. violence

3. By the 1850s, the Industrial Revolution had created

    A. restrictions on women's independence
    B. more scholarships for female students
    C. new opportunities for women to work
    D. the need for female soldiers in the army

4. What is the purpose of the bold headings throughout the passage?

    A. to highlight important dates in the women's suffrage movement
    B. to list the groups that helped Ohio women to gain equal rights
    C. to divide the information about Ohio women into three main sections
    D. to show how women's rights have declined in recent years

5. The original purpose of most women's clubs was to

   A. discuss literature
   B. hold weekly Bible readings
   C. reform education and medicine
   D. support the arts


6. Which statement is supported by the passage?

   A. Ohio women faced many difficulties in the battle for equal rights.
   B. Ohio women were unsupportive of the women's suffrage movement.
   C. Women's clubs did little to help women expand their lives outside the home.
   D. Women's clubs opposed the cultural ideals of moral and domestic perfection.


7. The author most likely wrote this passage to

   A. illustrate how Ohio women helped to support soldiers fighting in World War I
   B. show why Ohio women didn't think that abolition and suffrage were similar
   C. explain why Ohio women didn't want to work outside the home
   D. describe how life for Ohio women has changed over the years

8. Which factors had the greatest impact on Ohio women's social freedom? How were women affected? Use information from the passage to support your answer.

# EARTHQUAKES AND SEISMIC RISK IN OHIO
## by Michael C. Hansen

1     Most people do not think of Ohio as an earthquake-prone state. However, at least 120 earthquakes with epicenters in Ohio have been felt since 1776. In addition, a number of earthquakes with origins outside Ohio have been felt in the state. Most of these earthquakes have been felt only locally. These have caused no damage or injuries.

2     However, at least fourteen moderate-size earthquakes have caused minor to moderate damage in Ohio. Fortunately, no deaths and only a few minor injuries have been recorded for these events.

3     Ohio is on the periphery of the New Madrid Seismic Zone. That is an area in Missouri and adjacent states. It was the site of the largest earthquake sequence to occur in historical times in the continental United States. Four great earthquakes were part of a series at New Madrid in 1811 and 1812. These events were felt throughout the eastern United States. They were of sufficient intensity to topple chimneys in Cincinnati. Some estimates suggest that these earthquakes were in the range of 8.0 on the Richter scale.

4     A major earthquake centered near Charleston, South Carolina, in 1886 was strongly felt in Ohio. More recently, an earthquake with a Richter magnitude of 5.3 was centered at Sharpsburg, Kentucky, in 1980. It was strongly felt throughout Ohio. It caused minor to moderate damage in communities near the Ohio River in southwestern Ohio. In 1998, a 5.2-magnitude earthquake occurred in western Pennsylvania, just east of Ohio.

**Earthquake Regions**

5     Three areas of the state appear to be particularly susceptible to seismic activity.

6     Shelby County and [the] surrounding counties in western Ohio have experienced more earthquakes than any other area of the state. At least forty felt earthquakes have occurred in this area since 1875. Most of these events have caused little or no damage. Earthquakes in 1875, 1930, 1931, and 1937 caused minor to moderate damage. Two earthquakes in 1937, on March 2nd and March 9th, caused significant damage in the Shelby County community of Anna. The damage included toppled chimneys, cracked plaster, broken windows, and structural damage to buildings. The community school had to be razed because of structural damage. It was of brick construction.

7     Northeastern Ohio has experienced at least twenty felt earthquakes since 1836. Most of these events were small. They caused little or no damage. However, an earthquake on January 31, 1986, strongly shook Ohio. It was felt in ten other states and southern Canada. This event had a Richter magnitude of 5.0. It caused minor to moderate damage, including broken windows and cracked plaster, in the epicentral area of Lake and Geauga Counties.

8    Southeastern Ohio has been the site of at least ten felt earthquakes with epicenters in the state since 1776. The 1776 event, recorded by a Moravian missionary, has a very uncertain location. Earthquakes in 1901 near Portsmouth (Scioto County), in 1926 near Pomeroy (Meigs County), and in 1952 near Crooksville (Perry County) caused minor to moderate damage.

**Causes of Ohio Earthquakes**

9    The origins of Ohio earthquakes, as with earthquakes throughout the eastern United States, are poorly understood at this time. Those in Ohio appear to be associated with ancient zones of weakness in the Earth's crust. They formed during continental collision and mountain-building events about a billion years ago. These zones are characterized by deeply buried and poorly known faults. Some of these faults serve as the sites for periodic release of strain that is constantly building up in the North American continental plate due to continuous movement of the tectonic plates that make up the Earth's crust.

**Seismic Risk**

10    Seismic risk in Ohio, and the eastern United States in general, is difficult to evaluate. Earthquakes are generally infrequent in comparison to plate-margin areas such as California. Also, active faults do not reach the surface in Ohio. Therefore, they cannot be mapped without the aid of expensive subsurface techniques.

11    A great difficulty in predicting large earthquakes in the eastern United States is that the "recurrence interval"—the time between large earthquakes—is commonly very long. It is on the order of hundreds or even thousands of years. The historic record in most areas, including Ohio, is only on the order of about two hundred years. That is an instant, geologically speaking. It is nearly impossible to estimate either the maximum magnitude or the frequency of earthquakes at any particular site.

12    Earthquake risk in the eastern United States is further compounded by the fact that seismic waves tend to travel for very long distances. The relatively brittle and flat-lying sedimentary rocks of this region tend to carry these waves throughout an area of thousands of square miles for even a moderate-size earthquake. Damaging ground motion would occur in an area about ten times larger than for a California earthquake of comparable intensity.

13    An additional factor in earthquake risk is the nature of the geologic materials upon which a structure is built. Ground motion from seismic waves tends to be magnified by unconsolidated sediments, such as thick deposits of clay or sand and gravel. Such deposits are extensive in Ohio. Buildings constructed on bedrock tend to experience much less ground motion, and therefore less damage.

14    The brief historic record of Ohio earthquakes suggests a risk of moderately damaging earthquakes in the western, northeastern, and southeastern parts of the state. Whether these areas might produce larger, more damaging earthquakes is

currently unknown, but detailed geologic mapping, subsurface investigations, and seismic monitoring will greatly help in assessing the risk.

1. What is the purpose of the bold headings throughout the passage?

    A. to show readers what the author thinks of Ohio's seismic risk
    B. to make the passage easier for the reader to understand
    C. to list the areas that are at the most risk for earthquakes in Ohio
    D. to show why earthquakes can be very difficult to predict

2. According to the passage, the New Madrid Seismic Zone was

    A. the site of the most powerful earthquake felt anywhere on Earth
    B. an area where little or no seismic activity occurs
    C. an area of deeply buried and poorly known faults
    D. the site of the largest earthquake sequence to occur in the U.S.

3. "More recently, an earthquake with a Richter **magnitude** of 5.3 was centered at Sharpsburg, Kentucky, in 1980."

    What does the word **magnitude** mean?

    A. size
    B. time
    C. sheet
    D. plan

4. Which area of Ohio has experienced the most earthquakes?

    A. the Perry County region
    B. southeastern Ohio
    C. in and around Shelby County
    D. northeastern Ohio

5. Why does the author include information about earthquakes with epicenters in other states?

   A. to tell readers why Ohio needs a better earthquake warning system
   B. to warn readers about areas on the east coast that should be avoided
   C. to show that powerful earthquakes can be felt across many states
   D. to explain that Ohio experiences more earthquakes than the other states

6. What seems to be the cause of the earthquakes in Ohio?

   A. flat-lying sedimentary rocks
   B. a weakness in the Earth's crust
   C. large deposits of clay and gravel
   D. buildings constructed on bedrock

7. What makes it difficult to predict earthquakes in the eastern part of the United States?

   A. the long periods of time between earthquakes
   B. the fact that seismic waves travel long distances
   C. a number of subsurface investigations by scientists
   D. technology that can only detect large crust shifts

8. "Damaging ground motion would occur in an area about ten times larger than for a California earthquake of comparable **intensity**."

   What does the word **intensity**?

   A. length
   B. damage
   C. strength
   D. appeal

9. The author most likely wrote this passage to
    A. explain the history of seismic activity in Ohio
    B. show readers how to prepare for an earthquake
    C. tell readers why Ohio has never had an earthquake
    D. encourage people to move out of area of seismic risk

# JOHN PARKER OF RIPLEY, OHIO

1. Free blacks developed and nurtured the antislavery movement. Organized black abolitionists were speaking against African colonization efforts as early as 1817. By the decade of the 1830s, a vocal black press was addressing not only issues of slavery, but also those of race and civil rights for free blacks. These publications were supporting an increasingly radical campaign for immediately freeing the slaves.

2. African Americans were active participants in major national organizations such as the American Antislavery Society, which was established in 1833. By the decade of the 1840s, the rise of African-American leaders like Frederick Douglass reflected the increasing importance of former slaves in the antislavery crusade. They replaced the well-established free black elites who had dominated the movement in the first few decades of the nineteenth century. Ultimately, a growing militancy, race consciousness, and involvement in the national political arena would characterize the black antislavery movement through the period of the Civil War.

3. Free African Americans performed another important, though less well-known, function in the fight against slavery. They helped to secure freedom for many less fortunate than themselves.

4. John Parker of Ripley, Ohio, was a former slave. Parker was one of many African-American conductors on the "Underground Railroad" in the decades before the Civil War. His particular significance is magnified by the fact that his role is well documented both in local records and in his autobiographical reminiscences which were recorded before his death in 1900.

5. Although Parker's reputation is largely confined to the region of southwestern Ohio and northern Kentucky, his accomplishments—in the years prior to and during the Civil War—are significant in the context of the drive to abolish slavery in the United States. Parker was not an outspoken abolitionist among his peers. He appears never to have joined or participated in the activities of antislavery societies. He never achieved the notoriety of Harriet Tubman, Frederick Douglass, Sojourner Truth, or many of the other less-celebrated black abolitionists from New York, Philadelphia, Boston, and other large urban centers in the North. Rather, Parker's unflagging, and oftentimes heroic, efforts to rescue escaped slaves from the "borderlands" along the Ohio River underscore the major role played by African Americans not only as slaves and fugitives, but also as rescuers on the Underground Railroad.

6. After having obtained his own freedom, John Parker not only assisted escaped slaves en route to Canada, but also repeatedly snuck back into slave territory to free them and to lead them to safety. The John P. Parker House illustrates these achievements and the antislavery activities of this former slave, inventor, entreprencur, and conductor on the Underground Railroad. As far as can be determined, with only one exception, he did not hide escaping slaves at his Front Street property. Parker lived and worked here before the Civil War, residing at this site probably as early as 1853. It was from this location that he worked carefully—with great risk to his life and

property—with other Ripley abolitionists and conductors on the Underground Railroad.

7   Although his significance is derived from his role as a conductor on the Underground Railroad, John Parker's importance is further enhanced by his position in Ripley society as a noted businessman, inventor, and entrepreneur. Parker operated an iron foundry at this site from around 1853 until his death in 1900. He also developed and patented a number of inventions from this location. He is, in fact, notable for being one of the few African Americans who obtained U.S. patents for their inventions in the nineteenth century.


1. "Free blacks developed and nurtured the antislavery movement. Organized black **abolitionists** were speaking against African colonization efforts as early as 1817."

   The information in these sentences suggest that **abolitionists** were

   A. free European Americans
   B. people who once worked as slaves
   C. people who wanted to end slavery
   D. groups of organized speakers


2. John Parker and Frederick Douglass are alike in that they both

   A. fought in the Civil War
   B. previously worked as slaves
   C. were conductors on the Underground Railroad
   D. achieved fame while battling to end slavery


3. What is this passage mostly about?

   A. the purpose of the Underground Railroad
   B. the role former slaves played in ending slavery
   C. the effects of slavery in Kentucky and Ohio
   D. the accomplishments of John Parker

4. The author most likely included the information about John Parker sneaking back into slave territory to

   A. illustrate his commitment to ending slavery.
   B. prove that he was braver than Harriet Tubman.
   C. establish the important of the John P. Parker House.
   D. distinguish him from Frederick Douglass.

5. What does this passage suggest about John Parker?

   A. He was a timid person.
   B. He was a great hero.
   C. He was a good fighter.
   D. He was an excellent speaker.

6. The "John Parker of Ripley, Ohio" passage is most similar to

   A. an informational brochure
   B. an editorial in a newspaper
   C. a story in a magazine
   D. a biographical account

7. "Although his significance is derived from his role as a conductor on the Underground Railroad, John Parker's importance is further **enhanced** by his position in Ripley society as a noted businessman, inventor, and entrepreneur."

   What does the word **enhanced** mean?

   A. undermined
   B. posed a challenge
   C. made greater
   D. misjudged

8. How do the efforts of John Parker and Frederick Douglass in the fight to end slavery differ from each other? Use information from the passage to support your answer.

# IMMIGRATION AND ETHNIC HERITAGE IN OHIO

1. Immigration to Ohio in the second half of the nineteenth century was characterized by growing diversity. The significant migration trends of the first half of the century continued into the second half. At the same time, immigrant groups became increasingly varied, especially around the turn of the twentieth century.

2. German immigrants continued to come to Ohio in large numbers. They set the cultural tone for many communities throughout the state. Cincinnati, in particular, was strongly influenced by its German population. The impact of their presence can be seen in a variety of areas. These include the support and cultivation of the arts, the endurance of German language instruction, the German press, and their influence on the city's political machinery. German Jews in Cincinnati were also quite influential in the city. This group was also the main force behind the development of Reform Judaism.

3. The Irish continued to come to Ohio in large numbers. They made up over thirteen percent of all immigrants by 1900. The Irish from this period of immigration were mostly Roman Catholic. They had a great deal of influence on parish life in their communities. Irish social life was also quite active. Many Irish societies and community celebrations were established.

4. British immigrant groups also made up a large portion of later nineteenth-century settlement in Ohio. The Welsh played an important role in the industrial development of Gallia and Jackson Counties. Many Welsh in the area were farmers. Others became involved in the growing charcoal iron industry of southern Ohio.

5. Toward the end of the century, the character of immigration to the United States began to change. Immigrants from eastern and southern Europe began to increase as a result of political and economic pressures overseas. Meanwhile, immigration from central and northern Europe began to level off and even to decline. With growing opportunities in the expanding economy of Ohio, the state experienced a rapid rise of new immigrant groups to the state, especially in the northeast.

6. Cleveland offers astonishing examples of the impact of turn-of-the-century immigration on Ohio. In 1900, seventy-five percent of the city's population was either foreign-born or first-generation descendants of the foreign-born. More than forty languages could be heard on the streets of Cleveland. At one time, Cleveland was said to host the largest Slovak community in the world and the second largest community of Hungarians. In addition, the city received a large number of Italians, Russians, and Poles.

7. Other Ohio cities, particularly Toledo and Youngstown, also experienced a rapid rise of Eastern European immigrant groups. Germans and Irish continued to dominate immigration to Cincinnati in the later decades of the century. The mix of groups

coming to the Queen City broadened, however. They now included significant numbers of Hungarians, Italians, and Greeks. Blacks migrating from southern regions also made up a significant portion of later nineteenth-century settlement. By 1900, 4.4 percent of Cincinnati's population was African-American.

8   Ethnic groups immigrating to Ohio were not always greeted with open arms. Anti-immigrant attitudes were strong in many cities. Riots occurred in Toledo in 1862. They were directed toward the city's African Americans. Their increasing presence was threatening to some white residents. In the mid-1850s, Cincinnati's Know-Nothing party and its anti-immigrant supporters threatened and intimidated German immigrants.

9   Ethnic strife also occurred between immigrant groups. For example, ethnic divisions within the Catholic Church created tensions over church leadership and the development of parishes in many Ohio cities. In Cleveland, the city's Hungarians wanted to erect a statue to honor Louis Kossuth. (He was the leader of the independence movement against the Austrian Hapsburgs.) The Slovak community in Cleveland regarded Kossuth as an oppressor. They protested strongly. The statue was not built.

10  The great strength of Ohio's ethnic history is that no one group grew to dominate the cultural landscape. Consequently, much of Ohio's diverse ethnic character has maintained its integrity over time. At the same time, particular ethnic traditions have increasingly become traditions celebrated by a larger and more varied population across the state. German singing traditions, for example, continue in Cincinnati's annual May Festival. St. Patrick's Day and St. David's Day are celebrated each year by more than just the Irish and the Welsh. The long-lasting heritage of Ohio's Amish and Mennonite immigrants can still be experienced in Holmes, Geauga, and Trumbull Counties. At the Slavic Village Harvest Festival in Cleveland, visitors can celebrate the cultural legacy of that city's large Polish community. These examples are just a small selection of cultural expressions that document Ohio's varied ethnic heritage.

1. German and Irish immigrants to Ohio were alike in that they both
   A. showed anti-immigrant attitudes toward Italians.
   B. insisted on the continued teaching of their native languages.
   C. used religion to influence their communities.
   D. helped in the development of Gallia and Jackson counties.

2. What is this passage mostly about?

   A. immigration trends throughout Ohio history
   B. the establishment of immigrant celebrations in Ohio
   C. the rise in the African-American population of Ohio
   D. problems between immigrants and native Ohioans

3. The author most likely wrote this passage in order to

   A. describe immigration patterns in Ohio today
   B. narrate a historical story set in an Ohio city
   C. persuade people to accept their ethnic differences
   D. explain the varied ethnic history of Ohio

4. The author most likely included the information in the last paragraph of the passage to

   A. give the population numbers for different ethnic groups in Ohio today
   B. persuade readers to attend some of Ohio's ethnic festivals
   C. show that Ohio's ethnic traditions continue in the present
   D. illustrate how different ethnic groups in Ohio continue to fight

5. "**Ethnic strife** also occurred between immigrant groups. For example, ethnic divisions within the Catholic Church created tensions over church leadership and the development of parishes in many Ohio cities."

   The information in these sentences suggests that **ethnic strife** was

   A. a lack of development in many Ohio cities
   B. a problem between people from different countries
   C. a change in the leadership of the Catholic Church
   D. a separation between church and city leaders

6. In the 1850s and 1860s, Germans and African Americans in Ohio were alike in that they both

   A. experienced decreases in their populations.
   B. faced threats from anti-immigrant supporters.
   C. held protests against the creation of a statue.
   D. greatly influenced the political machinery.

7. The "Immigration and Ethnic Heritage in Ohio" passage is most similar to

   A. a set of detailed instructions
   B. an article within a textbook
   C. a story within a magazine
   D. an editorial in a newspaper

8. The Slavic Village Harvest Festival takes place in

   A. Cincinnati.
   B. Cleveland.
   C. Youngstown.
   D. Toledo.

9. A statue honoring Louis Kossuth was not built because of protests by the

   A. Slovak community.
   B. Catholic Church.
   C. Italian immigrants.
   D. anti-immigrant supporters.

10. "The great strength of Ohio's ethnic history is that no one group grew to dominate the cultural landscape. Consequently, much of Ohio's diverse ethnic character has maintained its **integrity** over time."

    What does the word **integrity** mean?
    A. quantity
    B. development
    C. history
    D. genuineness

11. How were immigration in Cincinnati and immigration in Cleveland different from each other? Use information from the passage to support your answer.

# MUSKELLUNGE FISHING IN OHIO

1. The Ohio Department of Natural Resources Division of Wildlife's muskellunge program is designed to maintain high-quality muskellunge, or "muskie," fisheries at a limited number of lakes throughout Ohio. In selecting lakes for stocking, emphasis is placed upon keeping a relatively even distribution throughout the state so that all Ohioans can enjoy these fisheries. Water quality, habitat, food supply, and angler access are also important considerations.

2. Scientists reported Ohio's native muskellunge to be abundant as early as 1810. Muskies were an important commercial fish as late as 1930. After 1930, muskellunge populations declined significantly, especially in the Lake Erie drainage area. This had resulted from urbanization, blocking of migration routes by dams, and draining of vast marshlands for agriculture. Stream populations were severely limited by pollution, channelization, erosion, and the situations of spawning habitat. The species was hardly known to modern-day fishermen until the Division of Wildlife began its artificial breeding program in 1952.

3. The division first attempted to breed muskies in 1948. Native brood fish were trapped live from Ohio streams and placed in hatchery ponds at Kincaid Fish Farm, in hopes that natural reproduction would occur. Because of poor success with this project, an artificial breeding program was started. Success was achieved in 1953. Ten thousand fry were stocked in Rocky Fork Lake. As many as 2,265 fingerlings were stocked in nine selected lakes and streams.

4. Since then, the Division of Wildlife has greatly expanded its breeding and stocking program. In 1982, the division redirected its efforts to the production of eight- to ten-inch fish. Ongoing research was demonstrating that they survived better than three- to six-inch fish. As a result, opportunities for catching muskies are better in Ohio today than ever before.

5. Most Ohio muskies are caught from April through October when the water temperature varies from fifty-five to seventy-five degrees Fahrenheit. The best lakes to fish for muskellunge are Leesville, Clear Fork Reservoir, Salt Fork, West Branch, Alum Creek, Piedmont, Cowan, Milton, and Pymatuning. Good muskellunge streams are Paint Creek, Grand River, Sunfish Creek, Little Muskingum River, Rocky Fork Creek, Salt Creek, Wills Creek, and the Mahoning River. Some of these stream fisheries are dependent upon reservoir stocking within the same watershed.

6. Muskies will utilize shallow water habitat along shorelines and underwater humps and bars, such as weed beds and submerged trees, as long as the water temperature is below seventy-eight degrees Fahrenheit. Once the water temperature climbs above this temperature range—around mid-June—muskies follow their main food source (fish called "gizzard shad") out into the open lake away from the shallow water. Some muskies will return to the shallow water as the water cools down in September.

7   With the increased catch of muskellunge from Ohio waters, interest among fishermen grew and the Division of Wildlife needed to obtain information on the muskellunge harvest. Therefore, an organization was formed in 1961 to officially record the large muskies caught each year. The name "Ohio Huskie Muskie Club" seemed like a natural fit. The club fosters and promotes sport fishing for muskellunge and promotes the release of non-trophy (less than thirty-inch) muskies. They promote good sportsmanship and brotherhood among men, women, and children and provide the Division of Wildlife with statewide information on muskellunge catch and harvest.

8   The club has proven to be an excellent vehicle for obtaining information that is valuable in evaluating fish management activities and planning. Many states have copied Ohio's Huskie Muskie Club system to achieve the same results Ohio has enjoyed. Ohio ranks high among the states each year in total catch of muskellunge and, for the past several years, it has been among the leaders in size taken.

9   When you catch a muskellunge, you may qualify for membership in this prestigious club. Catching a muskellunge measuring at least forty-two inches long attains regular membership. Honorable Mention membership is achieved by catching a muskellunge measuring at least thirty inches long. (There is no weight requirement.) Anglers who catch and release ten or more muskellunge measuring at least thirty inches will receive an Honorable Mention Release plaque.

10  Applicants must register during the year in which the qualifying fish was taken. Regular and Honorable Mention entries must include a scale sample taken in accordance with the procedure described on the application form. It is equally important to submit applications and scale samples for all muskellunge less than 30 inches long that are caught and released. Application forms can be obtained at most marinas and bait dealers at Ohio lakes that have a muskellunge fishery.

11  Anglers who catch and register a Regular muskellunge, or who qualify for the Honorable Mention Release plaque, receive their certificate/plaque at the March awards banquet. Anglers who catch an Honorable Mention muskellunge receive their certificate by mail the following March or April.


1.  What is the main goal of the Ohio Department of Natural Resources' Division of Wildlife's muskellunge program?

    A. to ensure that all muskellunge in Ohio have enough food
    B. to make it possible for many people to fish for muskellunge
    C. to limit the number of lakes where people can find muskellunge
    D. to protect muskellunge so that no one will fish for them

2. "Because of poor success with this project, an artificial breeding program was started. Success was achieved in 1953. Ten thousand **fry** were stocked in Rocky Fork Lake."

   The information in these sentences suggests that a **fry** is

   A. a potato plant
   B. an everyday food
   C. a young fish
   D. a curious child

3. The population of muskellunge in the Lake Erie area decreased because

   A. the artificial breeding program didn't work
   B. people refused to return non-trophy fish to the lake
   C. muskellunge migration routes had been blocked by dams
   D. water temperatures fell below 78 degrees F.

4. What is this passage mostly about?

   A. how muskellunge populations in Ohio are regulated
   B. why muskellunge fishing has become a popular sport
   C. where the largest muskellunge in Ohio are located
   D. when muskellunge can be found in shallow waters

5. After natural reproduction did not occur at the Kincaid Fish Farm, the Ohio Department of Natural Resources

   A. trapped native brood fish in Ohio streams
   B. promoted sport fishing for muskellunge
   C. created an artificial breeding program
   D. released native brood fish into Ohio lakes

6. How are a nine-inch muskellunge and a four-inch muskellunge different from each other?

   A. The nine-inch muskellunge lives in warmer waters.
   B. The four-inch muskellunge has more offspring.
   C. The nine-inch muskellunge will survive longer.
   D. The four-inch muskellunge is considered a trophy.

7. The author most likely included the information in the first two paragraphs of the passage to

   A. establish the reasons for a muskellunge program.
   B. show muskellunge's role in lake environments.
   C. detail the muskellunge artificial breeding program.
   D. discuss the popularity of muskellunge fishing.

8. Which statement best describes the author's viewpoint about the Huskie Muskie Club?

   A. It is bad for muskellunge populations.
   B. It is a worthwhile organization.
   C. It is difficult to become a member.
   D. It is undeserving of its popularity.

9. When a person catches a muskellunge measuring at least 30 inches long, he or she qualifies for

   A. regular membership in the Huskie Muskie Club.
   B. honorable mention membership in the Huskie Muskie Club.
   C. an Honorable Mention Release plaque from the Huskie Muskie Club.
   D. a certificate from the Huskie Muskie Club.

10. Who is most likely the intended audience for this passage? Use two details from the passage to support your answer.

# AGRICULTURE IN OHIO

## County Agricultural Societies and the State Board of Agriculture

1   The first county agricultural society in Ohio was established in Marietta soon after settlement. It was modeled after societies in England and in the eastern United States. The purpose of the society was to encourage better farming through information sharing and competition. The societies held fairs and awarded prizes. In 1846, the General Assembly passed legislation that established a secure funding mechanism for county societies. This greatly encouraged their growth. By 1860, eighty-four of Ohio's eighty-eight counties had agricultural societies.

2   Also in 1846, the state legislature created the state Board of Agriculture. It was the forerunner of the present-day Department of Agriculture. Initially, the board's chief activity was to hold an annual convention. It was later assigned to organize the state fair. Cincinnati was the host city for the first state fair in 1850. Ohio was the second U.S. state to sponsor a state fair. For several years, the location of the fair moved around the state. The Ohio State Fair then found a permanent home in Columbus. Combining competition, education, and entertainment, the fair played an important role in the development of agriculture in Ohio.

## Twentieth-Century Agriculture

3   Governor James M. Cox served two terms, 1913–1915 and 1917–1921. He was influential in the advancement of scientific farming. Cox grew up on a farm. He hoped to encourage young people to stay on the farm instead of moving to the city. He increased state support for agricultural experiments and education, particularly in rural and village schools.

4   During the Great Depression, Ohio farmers struggled with severe droughts and erratic weather, in addition to the economic troubles common throughout the country. The Agriculture Adjustment Act of 1933 was passed during the administration of President Franklin D. Roosevelt. It created programs that increased the price of farm goods by limiting the amount on the market. Farm income rose significantly as a result. Three years later, the act was declared unconstitutional. The Depression-era Soil Conservation Act of 1936 helped Ohio farmers to replace soil-depleting crops with soil-enriching crops. At about the same time, the Rural Electrification Act brought electric power to many farmers for the first time.

5   Demand for farm goods skyrocketed during World War II. Production increased correspondingly. The labor shortage that resulted from farmers joining the military was in part eased by migrant workers from Mexico and the West Indies. Also, more than eight thousand German and Italian prisoners of war worked on farms and in food-processing plants in Bowling Green, Celina, Defiance, and other cities. Ohioans also planted Victory Gardens in their yards and/or communities to grow their own food. They did this so that farm produce could be sent overseas to feed soldiers and allies.

6   After World War II, many Ohio farmers were able to invest in mechanized equipment. These included twine binders, self-propelled combines, corn pickers, and tractors. These greatly improved efficiency. The percentage of farms that had electric power increased through the 1940s. That also boosted productivity. In the late 1960s, soybeans were introduced in Ohio. They quickly joined corn as one of the top crops grown in the state.

7   The second half of the twentieth century witnessed a decline in the number of Ohioans involved in agriculture. Dropping prices and a rising cost of living pushed Ohioans into non-agricultural jobs in cities and suburbs. Many of those who remained on the farm had to take second jobs to make ends meet. Both the number of farmers and the percentage of Ohio residents who were farmers have grown smaller since the mid-twentieth century. On the other hand, the average farm size and output increased. Despite the encroachment of cities and suburbs on farms, almost half of Ohio's land is used for farming. Agriculture remains a dominant force in the state's economy.

1. How is the information in this passage organized?

   A. An explanation of farming problems is followed by possible solutions.
   B. A description of farming in Ohio is presented in chronological order.
   C. A theory of why farming declined is followed by factual evidence.
   D. An opinion about Ohio farms is supported with researched facts.

2. "Despite the **encroachment** of cities and suburbs on farms, almost half of Ohio's land is used for farming. Agriculture remains a dominant force in the state's economy."

   What does the word **encroachment** mean?

   A. intrusion
   B. judgment
   C. measurement
   D. compliment

3. Farms produced more food in the years following World War II because

   A. more farmers employed prisoners of war on their farms.
   B. the amount of land reserved for farming increased greatly.
   C. more farmers used automatic equipment and electricity.
   D. the number of people producing their own food grew rapidly.

4. What does this passage suggest about Ohio farms?

   A. They are supported by most active agricultural societies in the country.
   B. They are usually the first farms to try new equipment and techniques.
   C. They produce more food than any other state in the United States.
   D. They are still important to the growth and development of Ohio.

5. The author most likely wrote this passage in order to

   A. persuade more young people to take up farming.
   B. inform about the history of farming in Ohio.
   C. narrate a story about a farmer who lived in Ohio.
   D. teach scientific farming techniques to new farmers.

6. During World War II, how was much of the food grown on Ohio farms used?

   A. to feed German and Italian prisoners of war
   B. to feed migrant workers from Mexico
   C. to feed workers in food-processing plants
   D. to feed soldiers and allies overseas

7. What does this passage suggest about Governor James M. Cox?

   A. He farmed while he was governor.
   B. He once owned his own farm.
   C. He knew little about farming.
   D. He wanted to help farmers.

8. How did agriculture remain a dominant force in Ohio's economy if many farmers had to quit farming or take second jobs to make ends meet? Use information from the passage to support your answer.

# TEMPERANCE AND PROHIBITION IN OHIO

1. Early Ohioans relied on alcohol as a beverage due to a lack of suitable drinking water. Farmers often distilled their crops in alcohol, which was an economical way to ship it to market. Since alcohol was so widely used, many nineteenth-century Americans fell prey to the evil effects of the "Demon Rum," as temperance advocates called it.

2. The term, "temperance," encompassed a number of viewpoints. Moderate advocates called for a more "temperate" use of alcohol. The most extreme faction wished to completely prohibit the sale and consumption of alcohol. Countless temperance societies were formed around the state in the nineteenth century. Women were particularly active in the temperance movement. Because their legal status made them completely dependent on the men around them, an alcoholic father or husband could make a woman's life miserable.

3. In December 1873, Dr. Dio Lewis spoke on the evils of liquor in Hillsboro and at Washington Court House. The Women's Christian Temperance Union (WCTU) was founded as a result. Soon, typically quiet women in those towns began protesting outside of saloons by praying and singing hymns. Eventually, the crusade spread to all parts of the state. In some areas, the women were successful in closing saloons, but they faced mobs and arrest in others. In November 1874, the national WCTU was formed in Cleveland.

4. Temperance was also an important issue in nineteenth-century politics. Nativists favored native-born citizens over foreign-born immigrants. They frequently cited immigrants' fondness for alcohol as a justification for limiting their political privileges. During the 1850s, German immigrants and the anti-immigrant Know-Nothing Party clashed over Sunday closing laws. These laws prevented the Germans from continuing the tradition that they had enjoyed in their homeland: visiting beer gardens on the Sabbath.

5. Whether to be "wet" or "dry" (to allow sale and consumption of liquor or to ban it) was a major political issue that was carried over from the nineteenth century into the twentieth century. When Ohioans had a chance to vote on the question in 1918, Prohibitionists won by a margin of almost twenty-six thousand votes.

6. In 1919, the National Prohibition Enforcement Act was passed. It imposed penalties for the manufacture, sale, and transportation of alcohol. The act went into effect as the 18th Amendment in 1920. The passage of this bill may have been influenced by the aggressive lobbying efforts of the Anti-Saloon League, which was founded in Oberlin in 1893. In fact, in 1924, nineteen of twenty-two Ohio congressmen considered themselves "drys."

7. Not all Ohioans obeyed Prohibition laws, however. Many people began to produce their own alcohol in bathtubs or they consumed alcoholic drinks in "speakeasies" (illegal bars). Authorities were unable to control illegal alcohol production and sales.

Bribes were often made to law enforcement officers to reduce the number of raids. The Great Depression also began to overshadow the Prohibition issue.

8   By 1933, a federal law was enacted that allowed for the sale of 3.2%-alcohol beer. In December 1933, the 21st Amendment was declared ratified. It overturned the 18th Amendment and ended Prohibition.

1. The "Temperance and Prohibition in Ohio" passage is most similar to

    A. an advertisement in a magazine
    B. an informational brochure
    C. an editorial in a newspaper
    D. an article in a history book

2. Early Ohioans drank alcohol because

    A. it was easier to transport than water
    B. it cost much less than water did
    C. they had no good water to drink
    D. they lived in a "dry" area of the country

3. As members of the Women's Christian Temperance Union, how did women help to change the alcohol laws?

    A. They transported alcohol in new ways.
    B. They protested outside of saloons.
    C. They voted in favor of Prohibition.
    D. They refused to sell alcohol to anyone.

4. While the 18th Amendment was in effect, some people

    A. created stricter alcohol laws.
    B. produced their own alcohol.
    C. bought alcohol at the market.
    D. distilled their crops in alcohol.

5. What is this passage mostly about?

   A. the movement to ban alcohol in Ohio
   B. the Great Depression's effect on Prohibition
   C. "dry" counties throughout Ohio
   D. overturning the 18th Amendment

6. What made it legal to sell, produce, and consume alcohol again?

   A. National Prohibition Enforcement Act
   B. Anti-Saloon League
   C. 18th Amendment
   D. 21st Amendment

7. Why did many Ohio congressmen most likely support Prohibition? Use information from the passage to support your answer.

# IMPROVING LAKE ERIE

1. Ohio's 262-mile Lake Erie shoreline is a great source of wealth for residents and visitors. Almost half of Ohio's citizens live within the Lake Erie basin. They enjoy its many natural, scenic, and economic benefits every day. In fact, Lake Erie has rapidly become one of Ohio's most popular visitor destinations.

2. The Ohio Department of Development estimates that the shoreline brings more than $2.5 billion per year in travel revenue to Ohio's economy. That represents a third of the state's travel revenue. Ohio's Lake Erie shoreline is certainly a resource worth protecting and improving.

3. Much of northern Ohio's economy is strongly influenced by the quality of Lake Erie's waters. In fact, we've seen the increased cleanliness of Lake Erie create an explosion of tourism. For example, the number of licensed charter fishing captains has increased from thirty-four in 1975 to nine hundred six in 2000. Recreational divers now explore historic shipwrecks once hidden by murky waters. Lake Erie has come a long way.

4. Lake Erie was once a popular national symbol of our environment in crisis. Many reports from the past described Lake Erie as a "dead lake."

5. Between 1920 and 1950, rapid industrialization and constant agriculture resulted in huge amounts of phosphorus pouring into Lake Erie. This dramatically increased algae growth. Increased algae caused pea-green water, loss of oxygen, and frequent fish kills.

6. The long process of recovery began in the early 1970s. Congress enacted tough environmental laws. The Clean Water Act in particular focused on reducing water pollution from factories and other polluters.

7. The reduction of phosphorus from Ohio's waters is a spectacular example of pollution reduction; however, significant pollution problems remain, despite the improvements. Those who visit or live near Lake Erie often notice that, after a heavy rain, the lake water along the shore changes from clear to muddy brown. One might even find a favorite beach posted with warnings because of unsafe water quality.

8. Alteration of the natural structure of the lakeshore, river mouths, and wetlands also contribute to water quality problems. Dam construction and shoreline development cause such alteration. Significant stretches of numerous tributaries, many river mouths, and some near-shore areas within Lake Erie itself have contamination problems due to these impacts.

9. Agriculture occupies approximately seventy percent of the land use in the Lake Erie basin. It has a significant impact on the area's water quality. Although agriculture's widespread and noteworthy adoption of conservation practices has begun, significant opportunities for improvement remain.

1. Why is it so important to improve the quality of Lake Erie?

   A. Animals in Ohio will leave if Lake Erie is not clean.
   B. Ohio's economy depends on Lake Erie being clean.
   C. People in Ohio get most of their food from Lake Erie.
   D. Most of Ohio's history happened close to Lake Erie.

2. How can readers tell from the passage that more tourists are coming to Ohio?

   A. Lake Erie is cleaner.
   B. Lake Erie needs a dam.
   C. More fishing trips occur.
   D. The lake is brown after rain.

3. Why are divers just starting to plunge into historic shipwrecks?

   A. Until recently, the water was too dirty to see wreckages.
   B. In the past, no one was aware that the wreckages existed.
   C. Until now, the water was too dangerous to swim in.
   D. In the past, laws stopped people from diving.

4. What does this passage suggest about the Clean Water Act?

   A. Enabling the act has solved many of Ohio's problems.
   B. The act was never actually passed by Congress.
   C. The act was a mistake that caused harm to the lake and its inhabitants.
   D. The actions called for by the act have helped to improve Lake Erie.

5. "Lake Erie was once a popular national symbol of our environment in crisis. Many reports from the past described Lake Erie as a '**dead lake**.'"

   The author uses the phrase **"dead lake"** to show that Lake Erie

   A. is an old burial ground.
   B. was considered ruined.
   C. had a recent name change.
   D. has always been unclean.

6. Which of the following does not contribute to the bad water quality in Lake Erie?

   A. development
   B. agriculture
   C. education
   D. phosphorous

7. "Those who visit or live near Lake Erie often notice that, after a heavy rain, the lake water along the shore changes from clear to muddy brown. One might even find a favorite beach posted with warnings because of unsafe water quality."

   The author most likely included this statement to

   A. describe why people like Lake Erie.
   B. show that the lake still needs improvement.
   C. tell readers not to swim in Lake Erie.
   D. suggest that the lake has not gotten cleaner.

8. What can people do to help improve Lake Erie? Using information from the passage, describe two things people can do to help.

# ENTERTAINMENT AND LEISURE ACTIVITIES

1      Early Ohio settlers were often too busy building homes, clearing land, farming, or housekeeping to have fun. They did, however, combine work and play in the form of barn- or house-raisings, quilting bees, and corn huskings. Extended families, neighbors, and friends gathered to socialize while engaging in productive activities. At the end of the day, the hosts might offer a meal, dancing, or a musical performance. Children, when they had completed their chores, played with homemade toys. Visiting and entertaining guests were important diversions, but they were also necessary in areas where there were few hotels or restaurants.

2      As the state developed, Ohioans had more time for fun. They celebrated holidays, birthdays, engagements, weddings, and anniversaries. County and state fairs became popular. Manufacturers produced a wide range of toys, games, and equipment for leisure activities. Canals and railroads made travel convenient and created a market for resorts and such tourist attractions as museums. City and state parks and recreation areas were created.

3      Beginning in the middle of the eighteenth century, Ohioans also had more money to spend on entertainment, such as the theater. The state claims some important dramatic artists. Most notable was Charles Gayler. He was originally from Dayton. His play, "The Buckeye Gold Hunters" (1849), was a smash hit and ran for ten weeks at the National Theater in Cincinnati.

4      The number of theaters built in Ohio in the nineteenth century demonstrated a growing demand for theatrical entertainment. Again Cincinnati led the way. By 1860, there were three theaters and two music halls. By 1872, the city had two more theaters. Columbus built its first theater, Neil's Hall, in 1847. Cleveland nearly rivaled Cincinnati for a short time. It had three theaters, all built in the late 1840s.

5      In the closing decades of the nineteenth century, traveling shows such as circuses and acting companies were well attended. Buffalo Bill Cody's "Wild West Show" was one of the most successful. It featured Ohio native Annie Oakley. She amazed crowds with her impressively accurate shooting.

6      Beginning in the 1880s, the growth of public transportation helped to fuel the rise of amusement parks. Euclid Beach Park and Luna Park in Cleveland, Indianola Park in Columbus, Idora Park in Youngstown, Walbridge Park in Toledo, Meyer's Lake in Canton, and Coney Island in Cincinnati drew large numbers of visitors. Modeled on similar attractions in Europe, the parks offered rides, games, swimming, dancing, performances, electric lights, and food. Few of these early parks remain open. Ohioans still enjoy amusement parks. Cincinnati's King's Island, which opened in the early 1970s, continues to be a major tourist attraction today. Cedar Point, King's Island's main competitor, got its start as a resort in 1870.

7      Many zoos opened in Ohio as well. German immigrants in Cincinnati established a zoological garden there in 1875. Cleveland's Wade Park was a forerunner to

Cleveland Metroparks Zoo. It opened in 1882 on land donated to the city by wealthy industrialist Jeptha Wade. Toledo's zoo was launched in 1900. The Columbus Zoo was the second to be established in the city. It was founded in 1937. In addition to exhibits of native and exotic animals, most zoos also presented musical concerts.

1. "Visiting and entertaining guests were important **diversions**, but they were also necessary in areas where there were few hotels or restaurants."

   What does the word **diversions** mean?

   A. communities
   B. advantages
   C. distractions
   D. relationships

2. Which word best describes early Ohio settlers?

   A. jealous
   B. busy
   C. silly
   D. impolite

3. What caused amusement parks to become more successful?

   A. the growth of public transportation
   B. the invention of electric lights
   C. the development of theaters
   D. the popularity of Europe

4. What is this passage mostly about?

   A. famous people in Ohio
   B. how Ohioans have fun
   C. the history of Ohio's music
   D. when Ohio became a state

5. How is the information in this article organized?

   A. Questions about why tourists came to Ohio are followed by what they did when they arrived.
   B. An explanation of what people liked to do is followed by stories from historical documents.
   C. Questions about the earliest settlers in Ohio are followed by the history of Ohio's music.
   D. An explanation of how people used their time is followed by examples of entertainment.

6. How can readers tell that people in Ohio enjoyed theatrical entertainment?

   A. Many theaters were built.
   B. Many stage actors moved to Ohio.
   C. Many people worked at theaters.
   D. Many Ohioans wrote plays.

7. What first helped Ohio become a center for tourism?

   A. the building of canals and roads
   B. people visiting their families
   C. many famous people living there
   D. Ohioans writing famous plays

8. The author most likely included the information in the first paragraph to

   A. establish that most Ohioans were rich
   B. show how early Ohioans had fun
   C. suggest that early Ohioans were bored
   D. explain why people came to Ohio

9. "Extended families, neighbors, and friends gathered to **socialize** while engaging in productive activity."

   What does the word **socialize** mean?

   A. labor in an energetic way
   B. hunt with a single purpose
   C. interact in a friendly way
   D. disarm with flattery

10. Do you think that Ohio is a tourist destination today? Use information from the passage as well as your own experience to answer this question.

# WOMEN'S RIGHTS IN OHIO

1. Beginning in the mid-nineteenth century, Ohio women fought to improve their legal and political rights. Some women wanted the right to vote, although most women reformers were more concerned with basic liberties. At the time, wives had few rights. Husbands were the sole guardians of the children and could even give them away without their wives' consents. A husband controlled all of his wife's private property. A widow could inherit only one-third of her late husband's property unless she had children to support.

2. In 1850, the second National Women's Rights Convention was held in Salem, Ohio. The organizers hoped to include female suffrage in the Ohio Constitution of 1851, but their efforts were to no avail. The following year, former slave Sojourner Truth spoke out on the issue of women's rights during a meeting in Akron. Reacting to several arguments made by men against women's rights, Truth contradicted existing notions of womanhood in her speech, "Ain't I a Woman?" In 1852, the Ohio Women's Rights Association was formed in Massillon.

3. After the passage of the 15th Amendment (1870), which gave African-American men the right to vote, women's rights advocates placed greater emphasis on gaining the vote. Women organized to advocate for suffrage. They became known as "suffragists" or "suffragettes." By 1870, Ohio had thirty-one suffrage organizations.

4. Several attempts were made in Ohio to initiate women's suffrage. In 1874, suffragists nearly succeeded in passing an amendment to the Ohio constitution. In 1912, the Equal Suffrage and Elective Franchise Committee put the question to voters about whether or not to remove the phrase, "white male," from Section 1 Article V of the 1850 Ohio constitution, which refers to voting rights. The amendment failed by popular vote.

5. Despite defeat, support for women's suffrage remained strong. New publications and groups sprang up across the state. In 1917, the Reynolds Bill was proposed, which would have allowed women to vote in presidential elections. The bill was signed by Ohio Governor James Cox and passed by the Ohio Senate. A ruling by the Ohio attorney general stated that the issue must be submitted to voters. In late 1917, voters defeated the issue.

6. Although women's suffrage was an increasingly popular cause in the early 1900s, many groups still lobbied against it. One of the main opponents was the United States Brewers' Association. Members of the association stood to lose a great deal of money if the state banned alcohol. Prohibitionists had been long linked to woman's suffrage; the association did not support the woman's suffrage movement.

7. Despite such opposition, Congress called a special session to consider the suffrage issue in 1919. The result was the 19th Amendment to the U.S. Constitution, which affirmed "the right of citizens of the United States to vote shall not be denied or abridged by the United States or by any State on account of sex." Ohio became the

fifth state to approve the amendment. It also passed the Reynolds-Fouts Presidential Suffrage Bill along with it. This bill guaranteed women the right to vote in the 1920 election even if the other thirty-six states had not authorized the amendment. The amendment succeeded in increasing women's voice and role in politics. By 1922, the first women were elected to the Ohio general assembly, two had been elected to the Ohio Senate, and four were elected to the Ohio House.

8    In Ohio, Governor James Rhodes created a commission to examine the status of women in the state. The Ohio Governor's Committee on the Status of Women was created in 1966. In 1973, the Ohio General Assembly passed House Bill 610. It prohibited discrimination on the basis of sex in employment, public accommodations, and housing.


1. Most women's rights reformers were interested in guaranteeing women

    A. the right to own property.
    B. custody of their children.
    C. basic civil liberties.
    D. the right to vote.


2. "The organizers hoped to include female suffrage in the Ohio Constitution of 1851, but to no **avail**."

    What does the word **avail** mean?

    A. use
    B. purpose
    C. question
    D. justice


3. Sojourner Truth's speech mostly challenged

    A. the Ohio government to approve women's suffrage.
    B. people to see beyond traditional views of women.
    C. men to treat the women in their lives with respect.
    D. women to fight for better educational opportunities.

4. Women's rights advocates placed greater emphasis on gaining the vote after

   A. Sojourner Truth gave her speech.
   B. the Reynolds-Fouts Bill was proposed.
   C. the 15th Amendment was passed.
   D. James Rhodes was elected governor.

5. For what reason did the United States Brewers' Association oppose women's suffrage?

   A. They didn't want women to pick the president.
   B. They believed that women would take their jobs.
   C. They believed that women would vote to ban alcohol.
   D. They didn't want women to be educated.

6. What was the most likely reason for including information about the Reynolds-Fouts Presidential Suffrage Bill in the passage?

   A. to describe how it differed from the other amendments passed at the time
   B. to show that the government wanted women to vote in the 1920 election
   C. to tell readers why women were only allowed to vote in state elections
   D. to explain to readers why women were given limited voting rights in Ohio

7. Which statement is supported by the passage?

   A. The 19th Amendment allowed many women to go to school.
   B. The 19th Amendment gave women a voice in politics.
   C. The 19th Amendment allowed women to inherit private property.
   D. The 19th Amendment helped women to find work outside the home.

8. "In Ohio, Governor James Rhodes created a commission to examine the **status** of women in the state."

   What does the word **status** mean?

   A. position
   B. health
   C. happiness
   D. education

9. The author most likely wrote this passage to

   A. encourage readers to support women's suffrage
   B. describe the Ohio leaders who helped women gain equal rights
   C. identify the anxieties men had about giving women voting rights
   D. explain the history of women's suffrage in Ohio

10. Why do you think it took over one hundred years for women to gain the right to vote in Ohio? Use information from the passage to support your answer.

# SPORTS IN OHIO

1. Sports and athletic activities have played an important role in the lives of Ohioans since the state's settlement in the 1780s. Organized athletic activities began to develop as cities grew larger. Near the end of the nineteenth century, professional baseball and football teams were established and amateur sports clubs formed across the state.

2. Baseball was an important part of Ohio's early athletic history. The city of Cincinnati became a leader in the development of this sport. In 1866, the Cincinnati Live Oaks played the Brooklyn Eagles in Cincinnati's first inter-city match. The Queen City later established the nation's first professional baseball team, the Cincinnati Red Stockings. This team is now known as the Cincinnati Reds. In their first few seasons, the Red Stockings won one hundred thirty straight games.

3. Several of the Red Stockings' players, like pitcher Asa Brainard, became national sports celebrities. Brainard was so well regarded that top pitchers on the baseball teams of the 1870s were known as "Asa." (In time this was changed to "ace.")

4. The Cincinnati Red Stockings team was a charter member of the National League, which was formed in 1876. In 1919, the team won their first World Series. They would capture this title again in 1940, 1976, and 1990.

5. Another well-known Reds player was outfielder William Ellsworth Hoy. Hoy was the first hearing-impaired player in major league baseball. Because he could not hear the umpires' calls, the umpires began to use hand signals to indicate balls and strikes. These signals are still used during games today.

6. Cleveland soon followed Cincinnati's lead by establishing its own professional baseball team and joining the National League in the 1890s. Famous pitcher Denton "Cy" Young played for the Cleveland Spiders from 1890 to 1898. Every year, the best pitchers in the major leagues are honored with the Cy Young Award. Cleveland eventually joined the American League, where the team went through a series of nicknames. The team finally settled on the name "Indians" and went on to win the World Series in 1915, 1920, and 1948.

7. Many other Ohio players made lasting impression on the America's favorite pastime. Moses Walker became the first African American to play at a major league level after joining the Toledo Blue Stockings in 1884. Simpson Younger became the first African-American college baseball player when he played at Oberlin College in 1867. Stockdale, Ohio, native Branch Rickey played for Ohio Wesleyan University before becoming a professional scout and manager. He is also famous for hiring Jackie Robinson to play for the Brooklyn Dodgers in 1947, breaking the color barrier in modern major league baseball. Cincinnati native Pete Rose broke numerous major-league records, including Ty Cobb's record of career hits.

8   Football was another important sport in Ohio's history. Cleveland native John Heisman (for whom the Heisman trophy is named) was a pioneer in the sport. He coached at Oberlin College in 1892. He coined the term, "hike," which is still used today to signal the start of a play. Additionally, he lobbied for dividing football games into quarters and a rule allowing a forward pass. Originally designed as a student game, critics felt that football was "a foolish form of mass brutality." However, the sport became widely popular and by 1890, high schools and colleges throughout Ohio had teams. Rivalries between cities, such as Massillon and Canton, and states, such as Ohio and Michigan, began to take shape.

9   Professional teams were soon just as common as high school and college teams. Many cities had pro teams in the late nineteenth and early twentieth centuries. These included such well known names as the Columbus Panhandles, the Toledo Maroons, the Massillon Tigers, and the Canton Bulldogs. In Canton in 1920, the American Professional Football Conference was formed. This was the forerunner to the National Football League [NFL]. The city is also home to the national Pro Football Hall of Fame, which opened in 1963.

10  Ohio boasts two football legends: Paul Brown and Woody Hayes. Brown won national titles coaching college and professional teams. He was the namesake for Cleveland's NFL franchise. He also started the Cincinnati Bengals. Hayes coached at Ohio State University for twenty-eight years and was one of the most successful college coaches in history.

11  Other Ohio sports legends are sprinter Jesse Owens, golfer Jack Nicklaus, and racecar driver Bobby Rahal. Owens was a high school phenomenon in Cleveland and later went on to be a star athlete for Ohio State. He is best known for winning four gold medals at the 1936 Olympics in Berlin. Nicklaus is known as "the Golden Bear." He won a record twenty major championships and is considered one of the best golfers of all time. Racecar driver Rahal's impressive record of wins was highlighted by his victory in the Indianapolis 500 in 1986. After retiring from driving, he became a team owner.

1.  The "Sports in Ohio" passage is most similar to

    A.  a historical article
    B.  a set of game rules and regulations
    C.  a local sports report
    D.  an opinion column in the newspaper

2. What led to the development of organized sports activities in Ohio?

   A. fewer economic problems
   B. a decrease in jobs
   C. the growth of cities
   D. new national leagues

3. The Cincinnati Red Stockings were most famous for

   A. capturing the first World Series title
   B. being the first national baseball team
   C. changing their name several times
   D. establishing an award for pitchers

4. "Several of the Red Stockings' players, like pitcher Asa Brainard, became national sports **celebrities**."

   The word **celebrities** suggests that the players were

   A. talented.
   B. energetic.
   C. famous.
   D. conceited.

5. What is the most likely reason for including information about William Ellsworth Hoy in this passage?

   A. to describe how the game of football has changed
   B. to show how the color barrier was broken in baseball
   C. to explain why hand signals are used by umpires
   D. to give information about a famous football manager

6. The sport of football was originally

    A. played in city gymnasiums
    B. broken into three periods
    C. intended to replace baseball
    D. a game for students in school


7. Which statement best describes the author's opinion of John Heisman?

    A. He often disappointed his local fans.
    B. He helped to improve the sport of football.
    C. He wasn't as good as Jackie Robinson.
    D. He didn't deserve any of his awards.


8. "Owens was a high school **phenomenon** in Cleveland and later went on to be a star athlete for Ohio State."

    What does the word **phenomenon** mean?

    A. player
    B. wonder
    C. scholar
    D. runner

9. To what sport do you think Ohio has contributed the most? Why? Use information from the passage to support your answer.

# RUNNING BUFFALO CLOVER

1   Congress Green Cemetery in North Bend, Ohio, is not just the location of the William Henry Harrison Tomb. This unique cemetery is also the home to the endangered running buffalo clover. The cemetery is managed by the Ohio Historical Society. Along with the Fish and Wildlife Service [FWS], the historical society is working to improve the habitat for running buffalo clover on their property.

2   One of the major threats to this endangered plant is invasive, non-native plants. Congress Green Cemetery is no exception. At this site, Japanese honeysuckle, wintercreeper, and periwinkle threaten running buffalo clover. Control of these foreign species around endangered plants can be a difficult and tedious task.

3   An ambitious group of volunteers joined the FWS and the Ohio Historical Society to remove these dangerous plants from Congress Green. Rakes in tow, volunteers worked to pull up the ground cover around running buffalo clover sites.

4   We suspect that these efforts at Congress Green will be beneficial not only in reducing competition from non-native plants, but also by increasing clover germination. Running buffalo clover is adapted to periodic soil disturbance and raking may be just what the clover needs. Come spring, we hope to see new running buffalo clover plants growing in the cemetery!

5   Running buffalo clover is a perennial species. It has leaves divided into three leaflets. The white flower heads are about one inch wide and grow on stems that are two to eight inches long. Each flower head has two large opposite leaves below it on the flowering stem. In Ohio, running buffalo clover typically flowers during the month of May.

6   This species can be found in partially shaded woods, mowed areas such as lawns, parks and cemeteries, and along streams and trails. Running buffalo clover requires periodic disturbance and an open environment to successfully flourish. This sensitive plant cannot tolerate full sun, full shade, or severe disturbance. The original habitat for the species is believed to have been areas of rich soils between open forest and prairie. These areas were most likely maintained by the disturbance caused by bison. (In North America, buffalo are called "bison.")

7   The historic distribution of running buffalo clover includes the states of Ohio, West Virginia, Kentucky, Indiana, Illinois, Missouri, Kansas, and Arkansas. In Ohio, current populations of running buffalo clover are located in four counties in the southern part of the state.

8   Reasons for the decrease in running buffalo clover populations are unclear. The species may have depended on large herbivores like buffalo to periodically disturb areas and disperse its seeds. As bison were eliminated, the clover began to decline. Current threats to running buffalo clover include habitat destruction and loss, small

population sizes prone to extinction, unfavorable land management practices, and competition from non-native plants.

9   The recovery plan's criteria for downlisting running buffalo clover to threatened status includes the discovery or establishment of thirty self-sustaining, protected populations throughout the species range. Although more than thirty populations are now known, few can be considered protected. In Ohio, efforts are underway to establish consistent management strategies that may contribute to the species recovery.

1. What is the greatest threat to running buffalo clover?

    A. human interference
    B. non-native plants
    C. widespread pollution
    D. soil disturbance

2. Why might raking help running buffalo clover?

    A. Raking spreads the running buffalo clover's seeds.
    B. Running buffalo clover needs its soil disturbed.
    C. Raking removes non-native plants.
    D. Running buffalo clover needs little soil to grow.

3. "We suspect that these efforts at Congress Green will be beneficial not only in reducing competition from non-native plants, but also by increasing clover **germination**."

    What does the word **germination** mean?

    A. built-in protection
    B. beauty of form
    C. beginning of growth
    D. education in genetics

4. This passage suggests that the most likely cause for the decline in running buffalo clover was the

   A. elimination of bison.
   B. introduction of new plants
   C. harvesting of trees for wood
   D. increase in Ohio's population


5. Where would you be least likely to find running buffalo clover?

   A. in a wide open lot
   B. in a mowed lawn
   C. along a trail
   D. near a cemetery


6. The author most likely included the information in the last paragraph to

   A. explain why Ohio soil is ideal for running buffalo clover
   B. give reasons for running buffalo clover's decline in Ohio
   C. list the best places in Ohio to grow running buffalo clover
   D. show how Ohio plans to protect running buffalo clover


7. Who is most likely the intended audience for this passage?

   A. people concerned about the future of running buffalo clover
   B. people hoping to learn more about non-native plants in Ohio
   C. people studying the history of the buffalo in Ohio
   D. people who want to learn to grow running buffalo clover

8. Explain the relationship between bison and running buffalo clover. Use information from the passage to support your answer.

# FROM BICYCLES TO AIRPLANES

1. Between 1896 and 1907, the Wright brothers manufactured and sold hundreds of bicycles. This business had given Wilbur and Orville more than just the wherewithal to build and test their experimental flying machines. Their experience in bicycle building had provided them with the tools and skills that would be required in the construction of an airplane. In fact, many early aviation enthusiasts predicted that the invention of a successful flying machine would be the work of bicycle makers.

2. After the line of Wright bicycles had been successfully introduced to the Dayton community, the brothers contemplated the aeronautical problems of human flight. Around this time, the brother learned of a tragedy. German engineer and aeronautical pioneer Otto Lilienthal had died in a glider accident. He had been the first man in the world to launch himself into the air and fly. This terrible incident inspired the brothers to work on overcoming the obstacles to human flight. As Wilbur remembered:

   > My own active interest in aeronautical problems dates back to the death of Lilienthal in 1896. The brief notice of his death which appeared in the telegraphic news at that time aroused a passive interest which had existed from my childhood. . . . As my brother soon became equally interested with myself, we soon passed from the reading to the thinking, and finally to the working stage.

3. From 1896, the Wrights began focusing their attention on the problems of mechanical and human flight. Time and again the Wrights returned to the study of Lilienthal's crash and the reasons for it. After all, the German pioneer had constructed wings that could carry him aloft. The problem had been his primitive weight-shifting technique. It had been inadequate to provide sufficient control over his machine. The Wrights believed that the machine should require the intervention of the pilot only when a change in direction or altitude was desired. The insistence of the Wright brothers that the pilot have complete and constant control over the balance and direction of the machine was their first major step toward success.

4. In Dayton, Ohio, the Wright brothers began their incredible journey into aviation. The bicycle business did more than just provide the funds necessary to pursue their interests in aviation. It also allowed them time, since the business was seasonal in nature. Bicycle manufacturing was the ideal preparation for engineering the structure of an aircraft. Weight control is a primary concern of both bicycle and aircraft designers, though for very different reasons. In the key areas of balance and control, the bicycle had helped to shape the Wright brothers' approach to aircraft design. In the fall of 1897, the Wrights shifted their operations to 1127 West Third Street. It was the final location of their bicycle enterprise. It was in this building that the brothers constructed their experimental gliders and later machines. They conducted much of their aeronautical research here. Here they built the world's first airplane. They successfully flew that airplane on December 17, 1903, at Kitty Hawk, North Carolina.

5    With their success at Kitty Hawk, the Wright brothers had proved that flight was possible. However, they needed to prove that flight was practical. For aviation to take its next steps, they needed a convenient, private place—a flying field—closer to home. Their experiments continued in an area of Ohio known as Huffman Prairie. Even though their first experiments at Huffman Prairie in 1904 were filled with frustration, their experience as bicycle makers helped them to master the mysteries of control and balance. Eventually, the brothers were able to stay in the air long enough to practice turns, circles, banking, and stalling. It was here that the brothers built the first practical airplane and learned to fly. They were no longer dependent on the wind and could take off and land when they pleased. The brothers could also stay in the air longer than ever before. By the end of 1905, the Wright Flyer III could fly twenty miles or more at a time. The Wright brothers had truly conquered the skies.

1. What had inspired the Wright brothers' to overcome the problems of human aviation?

   A.  their desire to travel cross country
   B.  their experiments with bicycles
   C.  Otto Lilienthal's glider crash
   D.  competition with other inventors

2. "After the line of Wright bicycles had been successfully introduced to the Dayton community, the brothers **contemplated** the aeronautical problems of human flight."

What does the word **contemplated** mean?

   A.  considered thoughtfully and deliberately
   B.  solved impetuously and hastily
   C.  arranged carefully and methodically
   D.  established attentively and completely

3. What does this passage suggest about the Wright brothers?

   A.  They were inconsiderate.
   B.  They were determined.
   C.  They were impatient.
   D.  They were amusing.

4. What was the problem with Otto Lilienthal's flying machine?

   A. The glider was too large to make wide turns.
   B. The plane was too small for the average pilot.
   C. The pilot did not have complete control.
   D. The pilot did not have proper landing gear.

5. What was the difference between the machine the Wright brothers flew at Kitty Hawk and the one they flew at Huffman Prairie?

   A. The plane flown at Kitty Hawk didn't depend on wind.
   B. The plane flown at Kitty Hawk was much less expensive.
   C. The plane flown at Huffman Prairie couldn't make turns.
   D. The plane flown at Huffman Prairie was more practical.

6. The author most likely wrote this passage to

   A. describe how the Wright brothers spent their time in Ohio
   B. explain how the Wright brothers solved aviation problems
   C. show readers how early aviators risked their lives to fly
   D. encourage readers to visit Kitty Hawk, North Carolina

7. Many early aviation enthusiasts predicted that the invention of a successful flying machine would be the work of bicycle makers. Why? Use information from the passage to support your answer.

# ALPHONSO AND WILLIAM HOWARD TAFT

1   Alphonso Taft moved to Cincinnati in 1838 from Vermont. He was one of a large number of ambitious young men from New England who sought greater economic opportunities in the boom cities of the U.S. West. Alphonso married in late 1853. His new bride, Louise Maria Torrey, was also from New England. On September 15, 1857, their son and the future president of the United States, William Howard, was born. William Howard was followed by Henry Waters, Horace Dutton, and finally, Frances Louise.

2   William Howard and his siblings grew up in the Mt. Auburn section of Cincinnati. The Taft family was an integral part of the social, intellectual, and political elite of Cincinnati, if not of Ohio. The Tafts hosted many well-known visitors. They participated in national movements, such as abolitionism. Discussions in the house focused on a wide range of topics. They covered national politics, social causes, and international events. In the house, the Tafts mingled with politicians, businessmen, and military leaders who later influenced the course of American history.

3   The home was also the setting for lessons for the Taft children. Here their characters and ambitions were shaped. Helen (Nellie) Herron, William Howard's wife, later observed the effect that the Taft parents had on their children. She wrote of the Tafts' confidence in their children, which pushed the latter to live up to their parents' expectations: "They [the Taft parents] had created an atmosphere in which the children absorbed high ideals and strove to meet the family standard of intellectual and moral effort."

4   Alphonso's first step as a public servant was taken late in 1865. He was appointed to the State Supreme Court. Later, he was elected to the position. In 1875, Alphonso became a candidate for governor of Ohio; however, he lost the Republican nomination to Rutherford B. Hayes. The following year, in 1876, he was named secretary of war and later attorney general in President Ulysses S. Grant's cabinet. In 1882, President Chester A. Arthur named Alphonso to the position of U.S. Minister to Austria-Hungary. In 1884, Alphonso became minister to Russia.

5   While Alphonso ascended the ladder of public service, his son William Howard grew up in Mt. Auburn. He attended Woodward High School. In 1874, he entered Yale College. After graduation from Yale, William Howard attended Cincinnati Law School. During his law school years, he lived with his parents. Soon after his admission to the Ohio bar, he was appointed the assistant prosecutor of Hamilton County. In 1886, William Howard married Nellie Herron. They settled in Walnut Hills, another of the hills that surrounded Cincinnati's central area.

6   William Howard Taft moved rapidly through positions of higher responsibility. He was judge of Cincinnati's Superior Court. He then was appointed solicitor general of the United States. He saw service on the Federal Circuit Court. He was governor general of the Philippine Islands and secretary of war in 1904 under President Theodore Roosevelt.

7    In 1908, Taft won the Republican nomination for the U.S. presidency. He then won the election. In 1912, Taft and Roosevelt had a falling out. Each ran for the presidency against Woodrow Wilson, thereby ensuring Wilson's victory. After leaving the White House, Taft returned to Yale as a professor of constitutional law. In 1921, President Warren G. Harding appointed Taft as chief justice of the United States Supreme Court. Thus, Taft was the only man in United States history to serve as head of those two branches of the federal government. William Howard Taft died in 1930.


1. "The Taft family was an **integral** part of the social, intellectual, and political elite of Cincinnati, if not of Ohio."

   In this sentence, what does the word **integral** mean?

   A. essential
   B. actual
   C. humane
   D. annoying


2. Why did Alphonso Taft move to Cincinnati?

   A. He wanted to be president of the United States.
   B. He wanted to take advantage of the financial opportunities.
   C. His wife was originally from Cincinnati, Ohio.
   D. His family wanted him to be educated in Cincinnati, Ohio.


3. What is this passage mostly about?

   A. why Alphonso Taft raised his kids in Ohio
   B. how William Howard Taft became president
   C. how the Tafts were active in the government
   D. why William Howard Taft lived in Walnut Hills

4. Which word best describes the Taft family?

   A. despised
   B. bashful
   C. inferior
   D. cultured


5. "In 1912, Taft and Roosevelt had a **falling out**. Each ran for the presidency against Woodrow Wilson, thereby ensuring Wilson's victory."

   The author uses the phrase **falling out** to show that Taft and Roosevelt had

   A. a quarrel
   B. an election
   C. a party
   D. an agreement


6. What does this passage suggest about Alphonso and Louise Maria Taft?

   A. They thought that the government was dishonest.
   B. They wanted their children to stay in Ohio.
   C. They had high expectations for their children.
   D. They protected their children from the news.

7. Do you think that the way that Alphonso and Louise Maria Taft raised their children helped William Howard Taft in his adulthood? Use information from the passage to support your answer.

8. Do you think that William Howard Taft would have achieved so much politically if his father had not been so prominent? Why or why not?

# LAKE ERIE WATER SNAKE

1. **Appearance:** Adult Lake Erie water snakes are uniformly gray in color or have incomplete band patterns. They resemble the closely related northern water snake, but they often lack the body markings, or have only a pale version of those patterns. Lake Erie water snakes grow to be from one and a half to three and a half feet long. They are not poisonous.

2. **Habitat:** The snakes live on the cliffs and rocky shorelines of limestone islands.

3. **Reproduction:** Young snakes are born from mid-August through September. The average litter size is twenty-three young.

4. **Feeding Habits:** The snakes feed on fish and amphibians.

5. **Range:** Lake Erie water snakes live on a group of limestone islands in western Lake Erie. The islands are located more than one mile from the Ohio and Canada mainlands. All Lake Erie water snakes found on those islands are protected under the Endangered Species Act. However, water snakes on the Ohio mainland, Mouse Island, and Johnson's Island are not protected under the Endangered Species Act.

**Why is the Lake Erie water snake threatened?**

6. **ERADICATION**—The snakes are often killed by humans.

7. **HABITAT LOSS**—Lake Erie water snakes have also declined because of destruction of their shoreline habitat by development and other shoreline alterations.

**What is being done to prevent the extinction of the Lake Erie water snake?**

8. **LISTING**—The Lake Erie water snake was added to the U.S. List of Endangered and Threatened Wildlife and Plants in 1999. It now receives the protection provided by the Endangered Species Act.

9. **RECOVERY PLAN**—Since the Lake Erie water snake has been declared a threatened species, the U.S. Fish and Wildlife Service (USFWS) must develop a recovery plan that describes actions needed to help the snake survive. The regional director signed the Recovery Plan for the federally-threatened Lake Erie water snake (LEWS). The recovery plan identifies actions and goals that must be achieved prior to removing the snake from the threatened species list.

10. The primary strategy for the recovery of the LEWS in the U.S. is to sustain multiple subpopulations of the snake. This includes a stable subpopulation of snakes on each of four U.S. islands in Lake Erie. This should help to save LEWS from humans. The

USFWS will also be continuing a vigorous outreach campaign targeting residents and visitors to the islands. The USFWS will encourage people to make changes on their land that will benefit snake habitats. It will conduct additional research for other potential threats to the continuing existence of the LEWS population.

11  Recovery of the snake will be deemed accomplished when a minimum of 5,555 adult snakes exist on the nine U.S. islands combined for six or more consecutive years. There must be at least nine hundred snakes on Kelleys Island, eight hundred fifty snakes on South Bass Island, six hundred twenty snakes on Middle Bass Island, and four hundred ten snakes on North Bass Island. The remaining snakes may occur on any of the nine islands. Finally, analysis of public attitude must indicate that human persecution is no longer a threat to the continued existence of the snake. Accidental human-induced mortality should no longer pose a significant threat to the population.

12  **RESEARCH**—Researchers are studying the Lake Erie water snake to find the best way to manage for the snake and its habitat.

13  **HABITAT PROTECTION**—Where possible, the snake's habitat will be protected and improved.

14  **COMMUNITY INVOLVEMENT**—U.S. Fish and Wildlife Service personnel are working with local communities to develop programs that benefit both the community and the snake.

15  **PUBLIC EDUCATION**—Public education programs are being conducted to raise awareness of the snake's plight.


1. What is the purpose of the bold headings throughout the passage?
    A. to suggest that readers only have to read some information
    B. to tell readers which information is important
    C. to help readers find specific information
    D. to show readers how to help the LEWS

2. How is the information in this passage organized?

   A. A story about the LEWS is followed by definitions of different laws about the LEWS.
   B. An argument for saving the LEWS is followed by several arguments against saving them.
   C. A description of the LEWS is followed by questions and answers about its situation.
   D. An explanation of the problem is followed by several solutions to rid Ohio of the LEWS.

3. Which word best describes the LEWS?

   A. extinct
   B. protected
   C. microscopic
   D. disagreeable

4. The author most likely wrote this passage in order to

   A. describe how people are saving the Lake Erie water snake
   B. suggest that the Lake Erie water snake be moved elsewhere
   C. demonstrate why people don't like the Lake Erie water snake
   D. tell readers that the Lake Erie water snake is a friendly animal

5. "The primary strategy for the recovery of the LEWS in the U.S. is to sustain multiple **subpopulations** of the snake."

   How does the prefix **sub-** change the meaning of the word **populations**?

   A. The prefix **sub-** changes the meaning to **quality population**.
   B. The prefix **sub-** changes the meaning to **single population**.
   C. The prefix **sub-** changes the meaning to **false population**.
   D. The prefix **sub-** changes the meaning to **smaller population**.

6. Do you like snakes? Do you think this kind of snake should be protected? Why or why not?

# THE OHIO MEMORY ONLINE SCRAPBOOK

1. Millions of people have called Ohio home since its creation in 1803 as the seventeenth state in the United States of America. Ohio's inhabitants include a multitude of well-known names. Ohio has produced such national leaders as Ulysses S. Grant and Gloria Steinem. It has nurtured writers, such as William Dean Howells and Toni Morrison. Among its native sons and daughters are artists and architects, such as George Bellows and Maya Lin; actors, such as Clark Gable and Paul Newman; inventors, such as the Wright Brothers and Thomas Edison; and athletes, such as Jesse Owens and Jack Nicklaus. "If I were to give a young man advice as to how he might succeed in life," Wilbur Wright said somewhat seriously in 1910, "I would say to him, pick out a good father and mother, and begin life in Ohio."

2. Of course, most of the people who have lived in Ohio are not famous. We will not find their names in books or engraved on monuments. Instead, we have to look for them in the often anonymous texture of ordinary life. Struggling to live on farms, in hundreds of small towns and suburbs, or in a handful of great cities sprawled around centers of commerce and industry, they have cared most consistently about family and friends.

3. The biggest challenge in engaging the past is that we do not know as much about it as we think we do. We sift through whatever the dead have left us—scraps of paper, letters, newspapers, faded pictures, pieces of pottery, houses, farm utensils, architecture, clothes, and tombstones. We discover that history is forever incomplete. We'll never really know what it was like to live in Ohio in 1850. We have to guess, to piece something together from the things people forget to throw away, the stuff in boxes piled in a corner in a basement or an attic. Can we trust what people tell us? Can letters or clothes or cooking utensils tell us things that were never intended about the people who created or used them? And how do we organize all these bits and pieces into a narrative of the past? How do we find patterns in the debris of human beings?

4. The "Ohio Memory Online Scrapbook" allows people of all backgrounds to experience history as a process, rather than to receive it as a product. No longer are the primary sources of history locked away in libraries with access limited only to those with the resources and energy to seek them out. The Ohio Historical Society—in cooperation with more than three hundred Ohio libraries, museums, historical societies, and archives—has used the occasion of the state's bicentennial to create a database accessible to anyone with Internet access.

5. The Ohio Memory Online Scrapbook brings together raw materials into a huge scrapbook. It is a virtual attic of the state's past. You can experience for yourself the excitement of studying handwriting, interpreting a photograph's images, or humming the melody of a song from tattered sheet music. You can get to know people from the past on their own terms. You can meet them yourself. Most importantly, you can ask your own questions of them. You don't need historians to tell you what to think anymore. You can do it yourself.

6   Take baseball: In the decades following the Civil War, baseball's popularity swept the United States, especially in the urban north. It became a professional sport and attracted the participation of hundreds of thousands of people. Want to know more about it? Just type "baseball" into the search engine. You will find photographs of both the 1869 Cincinnati Red Stockings and the 1869 Antioch Baseball Club. You can examine an 1894 scorebook from the Cincinnati Base Ball Club. You will find an 1845 Cleveland law banning baseball. The handwritten document reads:

> Be it ordained by the City Council of Cleveland that from and after this date it shall be unlawful for any person or persons to play at any game of Ball or at any other game or pastime whereby the grass or grounds of any Public place or square shall be defaced or injured.

7   Anyone convicted of such a crime would be subject to a fine of no less than $5, although the exact amount would be determined by the mayor. Perhaps you'll wonder why the Cleveland council felt it needed to prohibit something that we consider as American as apple pie. Why did they think that baseball was dangerous? What does the law tell us about the popularity of the sport? How, where, and by whom was the game being played in the 1840s?

8   Maybe you're interested in the history of African Americans. The Ohio Memory Online Scrapbook gives you direct access to documents and photographs that permit you to ask your own questions and draw your own conclusions. Here you will see Benjamin W. Arnett. He was a bishop in the African Methodist Episcopal Church and he lived in several Ohio cities. He became one of the most prominent black leaders in Ohio. There is a picture of the 5th Regiment, United States Colored Troops, posing on Sandusky Street in Delaware, Ohio. Lew and Ben Snowden were popular entertainers in central Ohio in the second half of the nineteenth century. They are photographed playing a banjo and fiddle.

9   Then there are matters of weather, clothes, and houses. These are the kinds of details that filled people's lives but often get left out of history that concentrates on politics, agriculture, and industry. Look at numerous photographs of the 1884 flood in and around Cincinnati. Learn about a small earthquake in Canton in 1820. Examine weather reports from the 1830s. Study the wrought-iron eagle weather vane that crowned the first state capitol building in Chillicothe.

10  If there is plenty to amuse in the Ohio Memory Online Scrapbook, there is also plenty to ponder. While you chart your own course through the state's history, you might also do some of the things that professional historians do. Think about the ways in which all these bits of information fit together. Look for patterns by putting together a wide variety of images. Ask larger questions about the development of Ohio, its future as well as its past. Consider the extent to which history helps us think about who we are and where we want to go. In playing with fragments of our past, you will experience the joy of making history seem alive again.

1. "How do we find patterns in the **debris** of human beings?"

   What does the word **debris** mean?

   A. trash
   B. writings
   C. culture
   D. dialogue

2. The author most likely wrote this passage in order to

   A. tell people about odd laws in the Ohio Memory Online Scrapbook
   B. get people interested in the Ohio Memory Online Scrapbook
   C. suggest that we do not preserve history well enough
   D. encourage people not to throw away their belongings

3. The "Ohio Memory Online Scrapbook" passage is most similar to

   A. an informational brochure
   B. an editorial in a local newspaper
   C. a set of detailed instructions
   D. a school class schedule

4. "Instead, we have to look for them in the often **anonymous** texture of ordinary life."

   What does the word **anonymous** mean?

   A. unique
   B. nameless
   C. restless
   D. preferable

5. Which statement best describes the author's viewpoint about the Ohio Memory Online Scrapbook?

    A. It is just like reading history from a textbook.
    B. It needs more donations to be incredible.
    C. It should be available to more people.
    D. It is a good resource for people who like history.

6. What does this passage suggest about people from Ohio?

    A. Most of them are famous.
    B. They like to study history.
    C. Many of them are interesting.
    D. They want to be well-known.

7. Who is most likely the intended audience for this passage?

    A. people from Ohio
    B. people who are in the Ohio Memory Online Scrapbook
    C. children worldwide
    D. professional historians from all around the United States

8. Do you think that you would enjoy looking through the Ohio Memory Online Scrapbook? Why or why not? If you did look through it, what would you look for? What would you like to know more about?

# TEAYS RIVER

1. Two million years ago, ancient Ohio's landscape was dominated by a mighty river. It rivaled the majestic Nile in length and grandeur. The prehistoric Teays River flowed for nearly one thousand miles. Its headwaters were the streams that drained the newly formed Appalachian Mountains. The channel they carved began in the Blue Ridge in North Carolina. It flowed northerly across Virginia and into West Virginia. It cut across the tip of Kentucky. It entered Ohio at Portsmouth. It then took a sharp northerly turn to Chillicothe, cutting cross-country to the vicinity of modern-day Grand Lake St. Marys. It then moved westward to Illinois, dipping south to St. Louis, Missouri, and emptying into an ancient northern arm of the Gulf of Mexico that once extended into what is now southern Illinois.

2. Amazingly, this swift-moving watery ancestor of the Mississippi and Ohio Rivers disappeared two million years ago after losing the battle with lumbering sheets of ice. Although it is long gone, the Teays River still affects life today. Its deep ancient bed, filled with sand and gravel, now yields abundant fresh water from wells. Many communities lying atop the buried Teays River channel tap into sand and gravel aquifers several hundred feet below ground for their municipal water supplies.

3. The extinct Teays River is credited with boosting the biological diversity of southern Ohio, and isolating rare populations of cave crickets. Shawnee State Forest harbors small, isolated patches of several Appalachian plants far to the north of their native ranges. They are believed to have hitchhiked downstream on the Teays from their North Carolina habitat before the Ice Age. Populations of the Ohio cave beetle and the Kramer's cave beetle in Adams County, which are endangered species in Ohio, are the only known specimens north of the Ohio River. These beetles were most likely stranded in Adams County caves when the interconnected cave systems of Kentucky and southern Ohio were separated after the Teays River dramatically changed course.

4. The formation of the Teays River took place about five million years ago during the Tertiary period of the Cenozoic era, after the age of the dinosaurs. Extensive systems of streams began to carve the mountains and dissect the plains, eventually cutting the great winding channel of the Teays River. Obeying its natural tendency to seek lower ground, the water flowed south to north, east to west, until it found its ultimate outlet in the young Gulf of Mexico, which had lapped up over several southern states in a thick finger that traces today's Mississippi River channel. Over time, the Teays River widened and deepened its channel. At the height of its glory, the sprawling watercourse varied from one to two miles wide, with depths ranging up to five hundred feet.

5. The heyday of the Teays coincided with the rise of the mammals during the Pliocene epoch at the tail end of the Cenozoic. By that time, Ohio had drifted into temperate latitudes. The climate was still warmer than today, with little seasonal variation. Although the fossil record from this time period is sparse, we do have some clues about life along the Teays from ancient pollen grains found in the Teays valley

sediments, as well as archaic bones dredged from a sinkhole in Indiana. The lush banks of the Teays would have been lined with a variety of complex flowering plants resembling the deciduous trees, shrubs, and grasses we know today. Beside the oasis was a mix of prairies and forests that would have hosted an incredible array of wildlife. Herds of the ancestors of today's grassland grazers, like zebras and horses, shared the savannah with camels and rhinoceros. Fabled creatures like sabertooth cats, giant bears, and mastodons would have dwelt nearby in the primeval forest.

6   The demise of the Teays started almost two million years ago at the dawn of the Pleistocene era when, in response to the cooling of the earth's climate, continental glaciers slowly migrated south from Canada. When the mile-thick glacier reached the vicinity of present-day Chillicothe, it acted as an enormous dam. It blocked the flow of the Teays and flooded the area. The result was a large lake, nine hundred feet deep and seven thousand square miles in area. It was nearly two-thirds the size of Lake Erie. It covered parts of southern Ohio, Kentucky, and West Virginia. Lake Tight (named in honor of the Denison University professor, William G. Tight, who studied the Teays in the late 1800s) served as an Ice Age watering hole for about six thousand five hundred years. The waters of Lake Tight continued to rise and eventually to overflow, forming deep new drainage channels that, in some cases, directed the flow of water in the opposite direction from the original Teays River.

7   One lasting remnant of this vastly altered landscape in southern Ohio was the newly created channel of the Ohio River. After the advance of the initial (Nebraskan) glacier that blocked the Teays River, three additional glaciers advanced and retreated over the course of more than a million years, covering two-thirds of Ohio with ice. In addition to flattening the landscape in places and leaving mounds of debris in others, the later glaciers further modified drainage patterns to the northeast and southwest. They established the headwaters of the young Ohio River in western Pennsylvania. They carved the channel in its present location with southwesterly flow.

8   When the last of the Ice Age glaciers (Wisconsinan) finally retreated from Ohio, the Ohio River was flowing free. Much of the old Teays River valley had been buried under sand and gravel, several hundred feet deep in places.

9   The Teays River may hold some secrets that are yet to be discovered. Much of what we know about the Teays, including its precise course and probable fate, has been deduced from examining the depth and composition of sediments in glaciated areas, and piecing the results together with the visible evidence in unglaciated areas. Whatever future discoveries unearth about the mighty Teays, its legacy will certainly continue to enrich life along Ohio's ancient Nile.

1. What led to the disappearance of the Teays River?

   A. The Gulf of Mexico rose to meet the river.
   B. Canadian glaciers altered the flow of the river.
   C. Thick layers of sand and gravel filled the river in.
   D. The Mississippi River cut through the river.

2. What does this passage suggest about the Teays River?

   A. Professor William G. Tight learned everything about the river.
   B. The ancient river transformed into the present-day Ohio River.
   C. The river changed course when Ohio drifted to a warmer climate.
   D. Scientists will likely try to learn more about the ancient river.

3. "Extensive systems of streams began to carve the mountains and **dissect** the plains, eventually cutting the great winding channel of the Teays River."

   The information in this sentence suggests that to **dissect** something is to

   A. go around it
   B. cut into it
   C. jump over it
   D. move next to it

4. The Teays River is the ancestor of the

   A. Ohio and Mississippi Rivers
   B. Ohio and Missouri Rivers
   C. Great Lakes
   D. Mississippi and Missouri Rivers

5. How does the extinct Teays River influence the environment today?

   A. The river formed a 7,000-square-mile lake when blocked by a mile-thick glacier.
   B. The river allowed for a multitude of plant and animal life.
   C. Complex systems of streams carved out the extensive channel of the Teays River.
   D. The riverbed provides the fresh water that many communities depend on.

6. The author most likely wrote this passage in order to

   A. narrate a story about fabled animals in Ohio
   B. describe where Ohio communities get their water
   C. inform readers about the extinct Teays River in Ohio
   D. compare the Teays River to the Nile River

7. The author most likely included the information in the first paragraph of the passage to

   A. illustrate the extent of the Teays River
   B. explain the extinction of the Teays River
   C. describe the uses of the Teays River
   D. discuss the formation of the Teays River

8. How did the Ohio cave beetle and the Kramer's cave beetle become the only known specimens north of the Ohio River?

   A. They got trapped in glaciers that moved slowly across Ohio's plains.
   B. They got stranded when the Kentucky and Ohio cave systems separated.
   C. They followed the Mississippi River north to the Teays River.
   D. The moved to Ohio when the climate was warmer than it is today.

9. Describe the origins of the Ohio River and its headwaters. Use information from the passage to support your answer.

Made in the USA
Lexington, KY
21 July 2019